Higher Education

in the United States

A Summary View

FRANCIS M. ROGERS

PROFESSOR OF ROMANCE LANGUAGES AND
LITERATURES, HARVARD UNIVERSITY

THIRD EDITION, REVISED

HARVARD UNIVERSITY PRESS
CAMBRIDGE, MASSACHUSETTS
1960

Preface

This little book is the end-product of a decade of evolution of a series of lectures originally written in Portuguese and delivered in Brazil in 1950 under the auspices of the United States Department of State. Published in English by the Harvard University Press in 1952, the first printed version was subsequently published in Arabic, Chinese, French, German, Italian, and Spanish translations. A revised English version was distributed by the United States Information Agency in mimeographed form in 1957 and later published in Bengali, Japanese, Portuguese, and Spanish.

The materials for changes in the text have come from many sources: comments received concerning the published editions, extensive experience answering questions put to me following lectures to student and other groups in Andalusia, Coimbra, Martinique, Brazil again in 1959, and Lima both in 1954 and 1959, as well as by students and adult visitors from abroad at my own university, and the mere passage of time.

Inasmuch as higher education in the United States is exceedingly diversified, it is obviously impossible to compress into a few pages a detailed description which would take cognizance of the many different types of organization and the great variety of practices to be found in American colleges and universities. Moreover, education in the United States has now, more than ever before, become a subject of widespread public debate. Experimentation is rife, and many long-lasting changes in detail will undoubtedly be introduced in the near future. The following sections, which are primarily intended for readers unfamiliar with the American educational scene, in particular readers outside the United States, consequently outline only the broader features of the more stable elements of the system. They do not attempt to report current controversy.

Inevitably, the contents of this booklet are based in large part on the university which I know best, Harvard University. The opinions expressed are my own and do not necessarily represent the official opinions either of Harvard or of agencies of the United States Government. As my involvement in university administration has diminished considerably in the last five years, I have been more than ever dependent, for this third revised edition, on what I have learned, directly and indirectly, from my compatriots in higher education, particularly my colleagues at Harvard University. Whatever wisdom is distilled in these pages is theirs. The generalizations, the conclusions, the omissions, and possible factual errors are mine.

F. M. R.

Cambridge, Massachusetts
March 29, 1960

Contents

I. THE BASIC PHILOSOPHY OF HIGHER EDUCATION
IN THE UNITED STATES 1

II. THE ORGANIZATION OF AN AMERICAN UNIVERSITY . . 7

III. STUDENT LIFE IN AMERICAN COLLEGES AND
UNIVERSITIES 15

IV. CURRICULUM PROBLEMS IN AMERICAN LIBERAL-
ARTS COLLEGES 22

V. PERSONNEL PROBLEMS IN AMERICAN HIGHER
EDUCATION 30

VI. THE FINANCING OF HIGHER EDUCATION IN
THE UNITED STATES 44

VII. PROFESSIONAL TRAINING IN AMERICAN COLLEGES
AND UNIVERSITIES 50

VIII. THE UNIVERSITY LIBRARY IN THE UNITED STATES . . 56

IX. INTERUNIVERSITY ORGANIZATION IN THE
UNITED STATES 60

X. AMERICAN COLLEGES AND UNIVERSITIES AND
INTERNATIONAL STUDENT EXCHANGE 64

INDEX 69

I

The Basic Philosophy of Higher Education
in the United States

THE HISTORY of higher education in the United States reveals that the contemporary American university system is the result of a fusion of the continental European system of specialization and research with the English "college" system, in which education is broadly conceived and yet maintained at a high level of quality. The Americans have in recent years added something new, however, something that represents an outstanding difference between the present system and that of the past.

The new element is the notion of equality of educational opportunity, regardless of race, religion, color, national origin, sex, or financial resources. Space does not permit a historical study of this idea, nor of the social, economic, and political conditions that produced this change in the American system. It is sufficient to point out that the new philosophy has penetrated ever higher in the academic structure and is now quite generally accepted at the university level. Education is a right to which every young American with the necessary ability and the requisite willingness to work is entitled.

Belief in the doctrine of equality of educational opportunity is sincere; it is deeply rooted in the hearts of Americans. It is a doctrine of which they are truly proud and to which, on occasion, they do not hesitate to give legal status.

Thus in 1949 the legislature of the State of Massachusetts passed a Fair Educational Practices Act which begins:

It is hereby declared to be the policy of the commonwealth [state] that the American ideal of equality of opportunity requires that students, otherwise qualified, be admitted to educational institutions without regard to race, color, religion, creed or national origin, except that, with regard to religious or denominational educational institutions, students, otherwise qualified, shall have the equal opportunity to attend therein without discrimination because of race, color or national origin.

Massachusetts is not the only state to have passed such a law. New York and New Jersey have also done so.

In actual practice what does a law of this type mean? The Massachusetts law specifically states that "it shall be an unfair educational practice for an educational institution," any educational institution, be it nursery school or university, to discriminate against applicants for admission "because of race, religion, creed, color, or national origin," or "to cause to be made any written or oral inquiry concerning the race, religion, color, or national origin of a person seeking admission." By interpretation, the law further means that an educational institution, in the forms used by students to apply for admission, may not ask for information concerning the applicant's place of birth nor concerning his mother's maiden name; in the United States such information often discloses national origin. A law of this type, when combined with a large number of scholarships and fellowships for needy students, is very effective in advancing the notion of equality of educational opportunity. At the close of World War II and of the Korean conflict, the federal government passed laws assuring veterans of financial aid while attending colleges and universities and thus helped remove some of the financial barriers hindering the full extension of the American ideal.

In some sections of the United States, the implementation of the doctrine of equal educational opportunity has proceeded along special lines. In the South, for example, where a racial or color problem has long existed, the educational system is in a state of transition from a situation in which states endeavored to make available to the Negroes educational facilities that were equal to, although separate from, those available to the whites, to a situation in which the Negroes are admitted to the same schools as the whites.

The first consequence of the new philosophy in the United States is necessarily a great increase in the number of institutions of higher education, with all the problems of staff, libraries, laboratories, dormitories, dining halls, medical services, and the like that such expansion entails. There are thus in the United States today some 1,450 colleges and universities, 1,950 if the two-year junior or community colleges are included. Precise figures as reported by the United States Office of Education for the fall of 1958 follow.

	Number	Enrollment
Universities	141	1,436,000
Liberal arts colleges	789	909,000
Separately organized professional schools:		
Teachers colleges	197	323,000
Technological schools	46	97,000
Theological, religious	154	37,000
Other professional	127	70,000
Junior colleges	499	387,000
Totals	1,953	3,259,000

In this table, the phrase "separately organized" signifies not forming part of a university. In other words, superimposed on the elementary and secondary school system of twelve years' duration (thirteen, if the optional kindergarten is counted) are nearly 2,000 institutions of higher education. Attendance at them is completely voluntary, as compulsory education applies only to elementary and secondary schools. The laws concerning compulsory attendance vary by states. Provisions for exemption also vary, as does the enforcement of the laws. The majority of the states require attendance at school between the ages of seven and sixteen, others between eight and sixteen, still others between eight and eighteen.

Of the institutions of higher education, some are operated by the several states; some are municipal; many are private, including a large number that are church institutions, of different religions and sects. Slightly more than a third of all the institutions are publicly controlled; the rest are under private control. The public institutions enroll well over half the students. This considerable number of colleges and universities exists because the American public wants them, demands them, is willing to pay for them. In later chap-

RELATIONSHIP OF EDUCATIONAL INSTITUTIONS IN THE UNITED STATES

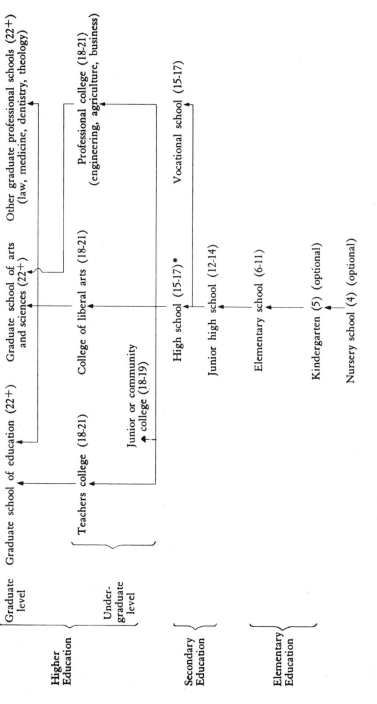

* A private high school which is primarily for students in residence is usually known as a "preparatory school."

NOTE: Figures indicate normal ages of students.

ters some of the organizational, personnel, and financial problems that are results of the expansion are discussed in detail.

In addition to this normal growth in higher education which has been going on for decades, there is at present a greatly increased number of children now in elementary and secondary schools. It is expected that a large proportion of these children, who represent the greatly increased birth-rate of the 1940's, will wish to enter institutions of higher education. In anticipation of a swollen enrollment in the colleges and universities, educators are giving considerable thought to means whereby the large number of students can be handled. A difficult element in the problem is the lack of certainty as to the duration of this abnormal increase in the number of students. As a result educational administrators are reluctant to assume commitments, especially long-range financial commitments, that might outlast the high enrollment.

A second consequence of the philosophy of ever-widening educational opportunities concerns changes in the curriculum and the danger of lowered standards. In an age in which relatively few persons went to the university and those few normally intended to enter the traditional professions, the curriculum followed by the students was simple and was more or less homogeneous throughout the country, indeed, throughout the Western world; it was a "classical" curriculum. In an enormous and complex educational system such as the one in existence today, a single curriculum is not adequate. There must be diversity. Some students do not want to learn foreign languages; others do not want mathematics; still others have little or no interest in the arts. Hence the necessity of developing a series of curricula that satisfy many different needs. To a certain extent the teaching staff loses control. The teacher must teach what the student demands. This is indeed a great change in the philosophy of education. Many educators believe that it is a great improvement. There is now a degree of competition among professors and among subjects.

These changes raise a very delicate question, a problem that symbolizes the new orientation in American higher education. It is the relation between teaching and research. The European tradition, which the United States adopted, requires that a university be a great research center and that a professor be an authority in his subject matter, an author of articles, monographs, books — in other words, that he be a specialist. This tradition was reinforced by the great expansion of science and technology. The tradition is now, however, in conflict with the need for teaching, for teaching effectively. Not all of the 1,950 institutions of higher education can be research centers. They can all be centers of good teaching. The graduate schools of arts and sciences, the normal sources of college and university teachers, have in the past prepared researchers, but as a matter of fact many, perhaps most, of the graduates of these schools who go into teaching have very little opportunity to do research. Almost all of them do teach, however. In order to teach effectively at the university level, they must be trained in the methods of research and in the use of primary sources and must be infused with the desire to teach from first-hand acquaintance with their materials. To expect more than a minority to become productive scholars is surely unrealistic.

Expansion in size together with

changes in the curriculum and the weakening of the research tradition can mean a lowering of academic standards. This is an ever-present danger in the United States today, for the whole concept of extending educational opportunities to ever greater numbers of students would meet with defeat if the education given those students were inferior in quality to what the chosen few used to receive.

A third consequence of the change in educational philosophy relates to the aims of the programs. In the past some of the universities tended to train an élite, to prepare the leaders of the various professions. The emphasis was almost always on the exceptional student. The teacher was often not interested in the intellectually inferior student. This attitude is still prevalent in some of the private universities. It is a natural attitude in view of the interest of the specialist in his specialty. In the past, and to a lesser degree at present, many of the students in such universities who were not academically first-class students already had an assured future because of family connections or personal wealth; the teaching staff did not have to be overly preoccupied with them. With the expansion in the numbers of students has come a change in the attitude concerning them. Not all of them, nor even the majority, can become leaders. The teachers now recognize this fact and organize courses specifically for the general education of ordinary citizens. The details cannot be discussed here. It can only be pointed out that this consequence of the new educational philosophy also brings its problems.

In order to exemplify one of the problems, the independent four-year liberal-arts college that aims to "prepare for life" might be mentioned. For the student who leaves such a college as a Bachelor of Arts and returns to his home town to enter his father's business, his education is often sufficient. But let it be supposed that the student wishes to enter a graduate school of arts and sciences or a graduate school of medicine. From the graduate-school point of view, he often does not have sufficient preparation. At times he is not admitted. If he is admitted, he may encounter grave difficulties. Such complications would be avoided if a college could be recognized as "terminal," that is, if it were stated forthrightly that the college prepares for life but not for advanced studies. This statement could not be made, however, in view of the notion of equality of educational opportunity, for the young twenty-one-year-old Bachelor of Arts or of Science should have an equal opportunity to go on regardless of whether he went to an independent college, or to a university college whose curriculum prepares specifically for graduate studies.

The inevitable result of such extensions of the ideal of equal educational opportunity is that graduate schools have to compromise, have to lower their admission standards. A concrete example is the requirement of foreign languages for graduate study. Thus for advanced studies in English literature a good American graduate school of arts and sciences requires a knowledge of Latin, French, and German. If the student, however brilliant, has not had adequate language training in high school and college, he must take elementary courses in foreign language while in the graduate school. What then exists is not a true graduate school, but rather a college for older students, with grave sociological consequences in many cases.

Higher education in the United States is thus in a state of flux. The best words for describing the educational situation at the present time are diversity and fluidity. The problems are enormous. The greatest amount of good will on the part of both teachers and administrators is necessary for their solution. Because of the changes that have been alluded to above, there are today two general types of great American universities.

One type comprises the private universities of venerable traditions, universities such as Harvard, Yale, Princeton, Columbia, Johns Hopkins, Northwestern, and Stanford. These universities preserve the notions of high-quality instruction, carefully selected student body, and more or less classical curriculum. They have one great defect: they are expensive. They depend to a large extent on the money that the students pay because they receive little or no money from public sources, although they receive large amounts from private philanthropy.

The other general type includes the state universities, subsidized by the states, consequently not so dependent on the money paid by the student, and therefore less expensive for the student. The list of universities of this type includes the Universities of California, Michigan, Wisconsin, and Minnesota, and Ohio State University. In these institutions there is necessarily a certain social if not political pressure which results in the offering of an enormous variety of courses adapted to the requirements of huge student bodies. The state universities are thus eminently successful in filling local needs as well

as being, in many cases, great national or international centers of scientific research.

The state universities wish to continue to function in this dual capacity, combining a purely state function with a contribution to education that transcends state lines. Consequently, many of their officials view with alarm any abnormal increase in the demand for higher education, as inevitably the state universities will in that event be under considerable pressure to cater to the youth of their own states first. This pressure has already taken the form of increasing the difference between the tuition paid by state residents and that paid by out-of-state students. In some states the latter pay five times the amount required of the former. This is a natural development from the point of view of the taxpayers. It is unhealthy educationally, for the state students are deprived of the valuable experience of association with students from other states.

The state universities follow the new philosophy of equality of opportunity. The private universities follow in part the former philosophy of high quality, of training the élite. Perhaps the best course for the future lies between the two types; indeed, some thinkers believe that inevitably there will be a union of the two. If that happens, higher education in the United States will be more fully capable of playing its part in a democratic society, educating citizens sufficiently for them to live a satisfying life in harmony with the common good, and training the leaders and specialists necessary for the protection and enlargement of this common good.

II

The Organization of an American University

PERHAPS THE most interesting feature of American university organization is its underlying philosophy. An American university is democratic so far as its teaching staff is concerned. The students, however, have little or no voice in the administration of the university. The present chapter will consequently stress these fundamental principles of organization.

University studies in the United States include the four-year "college" program, for which the bachelor's degree is normally awarded, and "graduate" programs which normally terminate with the master's degree, given for one year's study, and the doctorate, given for studies lasting four or more years which may or may not include the master's program. The college is thus an integral part of the university system and follows upon the twelve years of instruction in the elementary, junior high, and high schools.

A large proportion of the 1,950 institutions of higher education in the United States are the independent four-year liberal-arts colleges. They offer little if any instruction at the graduate level. These four-year colleges, which may perhaps be considered the backbone of the whole American system of higher education, are, or were at their inception, private; many of them are of religious origin and a large number continue to be church institutions. No further mention of them will be made here, but rather the more complex university organization will be discussed. The general organizational features described, however, usually apply to the independent colleges and technological and professional schools as well as to the component parts of a university.

A typical American university pattern includes a four-year liberal-arts college in which the bachelor's degree is earned — the "undergraduate" college — and a series of graduate schools which normally require the bachelor's degree as a prerequisite for admission — a law school, a medical school, a divinity or theological school, a graduate school of arts and sciences, and the like. A college that is part of a university is often called a "university college." The ensemble of the college and the graduate schools is called a university in American terminology.

A large number of American universities have undergraduate colleges or schools other than a college of liberal arts, or college of arts and sciences, as it is often termed. Thus they may have a college of business administration, a college of architecture, a college of agriculture, a college of physical education, a school of social work, a school of nursing, a school of music, or a college of home economics. A university may also have a college of engineering, although there are several famous independent engineering colleges, such as the Massachusetts and the California Institutes of Technology, that have nothing to do directly with any traditional university.

In some universities the term "graduate school" embraces all programs leading to advanced degrees, and not merely advanced programs in arts and sciences. In other universities the graduate school includes advanced programs in arts and sciences and in some other fields, such as education or business administration or engineering, but not, for example, the professional law or medical programs.

In addition to the normal pattern of one or more four-year undergraduate colleges and a series of graduate schools, other patterns are occasionally encountered. Thus the first two years of undergraduate work may be separated from the rest of the college and referred to as the "lower division," as distinguished from an upper or senior division. The liberal-arts portion of the George Washington University in the District of Columbia consists of a two-year junior college, a three-year college (Columbian College) granting bachelor's and master's degrees, and graduate programs leading to the doctorate.

The terms "college" and "graduate school" have been employed in a very restricted sense. In the United States "college" is the beginning of the system of higher education. In many Latin American and European countries, notably France, the *collège* is the end of the system of secondary education, equivalent to the *lycée* or to the German *Gymnasium*. The American college provides the basic university education, the graduate schools being for the most part strictly professional. Because the American student is in college at an older age than his European or Latin American counterpart, and because the professional medical and law schools are at a higher age level, the decision to enter such a professional school is perhaps more maturely reached. Consequently, Americans are much less apt to change professions than are persons trained in law or medicine in other countries.

The word "faculty" has not yet been employed. In many educational systems this word is used to indicate a school

such as, for instance, the Faculty of Law or the Faculty of Letters. In the United States the word "faculty" signifies not the school, a complete administrative entity, but rather the teaching staff of the school, whether it is an undergraduate college or a graduate school. Thus there may be a Law School and a Faculty of Law. The faculty would consist of the ensemble of the professors and be headed by a dean, who would at the same time be director of the school. There may also be a Faculty of Public Health, the faculty of the School of Public Health. In some institutions the dean of the faculty has almost no personal authority, except what is delegated to him by the faculty; he merely executes the legislation of the faculty. In others, however, the dean does have considerable authority, especially in matters concerning personnel and finances.

At times it happens that one and the same faculty serves as the teaching staff of more than one school. Thus, to cite Harvard University, the Faculty of Medicine is the teaching staff of the Medical School and of the School of Dental Medicine, a type of organization, incidentally, which reveals the Harvard philosophy concerning the teaching of dental medicine, which is conceived as a specialty within general medicine. In this case, each school has its head or director (the American term is "dean") and the Faculty of Medicine also has its dean, who is the same individual as the Dean of the Medical School. This arrangement is considered logical because the studies followed by both the medical and the dental students in their first two years are substantially the same.

This dual faculty role is perhaps normal in the United States in the case of a college of liberal arts and a graduate school of arts and sciences within the same university. There is a single faculty, the faculty of arts and sciences, which is responsible for the education of the students in both schools. With this organization there may be three deans, the dean of the faculty of arts and sciences, the dean of the undergraduate college of liberal arts, and the dean of the graduate school of arts and sciences. In those universities in which the faculty of arts and sciences is teaching on two levels, there is often a rather difficult problem to solve, a problem exemplified by the attitude of the students. The students in the undergraduate college accuse the faculty, that is, the professors, of being more interested in their specialties and in their graduate students than in them. The graduate students, that is, the students in the graduate school, accuse the faculty of spending too much time on the undergraduates and their multitudinous problems. The solution to this dilemma is not easy. An obvious although expensive solution would be the creation of two faculties, one for the college and one for the graduate school. Columbia University in the city of New York has done this, although with an inevitable overlapping between the two levels. Moreover, although, as has been stated, there are independent liberal-arts colleges, there are no independent graduate schools of arts and sciences. There have been such graduate schools in the past, notably at Clark University in Worcester, Massachusetts, and at the Johns Hopkins University in Baltimore, Maryland. For various reasons, some of them financial, these organizational experiments were apparently not successful.

Many American educators believe that there are great advantages inherent in the concept of a single faculty of arts and sciences. In the first place, more eminent scholars can be attracted if they have the opportunity to teach graduate students. Secondly, the quality of the material taught to the undergraduate is higher if the teacher is at the same time stimulated and challenged by the necessity of teaching graduate students and by a pressure to do productive research; any professor worthy of the name must know his subject at first hand and must know how to find personal solutions to problems which that subject presents. In the third place, graduate students have an opportunity of serving an apprenticeship in teaching and also of earning badly needed money if there are undergraduates to be taught, especially large numbers of undergraduates. Lastly, the contact with undergraduates, who are usually in quest of a broad, general education and a preparation for life and for the responsibilities of citizenship, is beneficial to the faculty members, who are thus prevented from becoming overspecialized. The latter should remember that, if they do not know how to disseminate the results of their research, these results are often lost. Undergraduate teaching requires a high order of popularization, either through lectures or through the writing of textbooks. Foreign professors within the arts and sciences who are invited to teach in American universities often find this twofold nature of their duties quite disconcerting, since it does not have an exact counterpart in, for example, continental European universities.

It was stated that a faculty is *responsible for* the education of its students. This is an indication of the role of a faculty in the universities. The faculty is often autonomous, independent, with authority in matters concerning educational policy and academic questions.

The faculty, through democratic processes, legislation, committees, and so on, sets the admission and the degree requirements, furnishes the instruction, and examines the students. It is even responsible for advising the students, but inasmuch as advising, especially those aspects of it that are not strictly academic, can be quite time consuming, there is a growing tendency to employ professionally trained advisers or counselors. In some institutions older students are used as advisers for the younger ones, and in a few women's colleges the "big-sister" or "grandmother" system is found. The big sister or grandmother is a third-year student assigned to introduce the entering first-year student to the intricacies of college life. The faculty, either as individuals or through a placement office under its supervision, may also assist students in obtaining employment after they have graduated.

A faculty, for example a faculty of arts and sciences, is often very large. The work of such a faculty would be impossible without subdivision. In some universities there is a major subdivision into the broad areas of learning. Thus at the University of Chicago these large units are called "divisions," Division of the Biological Sciences, Division of the Humanities, Division of the Physical Sciences, and Division of the Social Sciences. At Columbia University, within which the undergraduate Columbia College has its own faculty, there is a series of "Graduate Faculties," as they are known — the Faculty of Philosophy, the Faculty of Pure Science, and the Faculty of Political Science. Faculties, or divisions in those universities that have them, are traditionally divided into departments, each department corresponding to an academic discipline. The department is the basic administrative unit in a faculty, and therefore in a university. The department executes appropriate portions of the legislation of the whole faculty and also has legislative powers of its own. Thus the faculty determines the degree requirements in general terms while the department specifies the details. The department is a financial and budgetary unit and is also a social unit in the sense that each member of the faculty, even the dean, is normally a member of a department. The nomination of new teachers originates in departments and so does the promotion of members of the teaching staff.

The head of the department is often named by the dean of the faculty, although he is elected by the members of the department in some institutions. In many American universities the department head has little authority. He executes the legislation of the faculty and of the department. He is called the "chairman," that is, the presiding officer; occasionally he is called the "executive officer." In some universities, however, the department chairman has considerable power; he is called "head" and often retains the headship for years. On the other hand, the chairmanship may rotate, each chairman remaining in office for from three to five years. Thus each member of the department has the responsibility, and the work, at least once during his professional career. The burdensome duties are shared, and no one becomes an autocrat.

One conclusion that might be drawn from the foregoing paragraphs is that the organization of an American university is very rigid; there are traditional faculties and departments, with little possibility of adaptation to new conditions. In a certain sense this is true, yet here is not a weakness, but a great source of strength in the American organization. All the disciplines are protected and the organization is not subject to new fads and whims. A true university is a repository of all the knowledge already acquired by civilization. Its mission is to preserve this knowledge, to increase it through research, and to disseminate it through teaching. The university is impersonal, independent of the world. Farseeing educators want it to be so. They want to protect Sanskrit studies and atomic studies, belles-lettres and social psychology. The organization assures that all branches of knowledge are developed. In an age that stresses science and practical studies, the appointment of, for example, classical and medieval scholars is rendered certain. This remoteness from the world does not, of course, apply to individual faculty members, many of whom are active as consultants to government and industry, as described in Chapter V.

Yet at times it is necessary to develop new fields of study. The flexibility of the organization permits this. New interdisciplinary programs, such as social science, or the history of American civilization, or chemical physics, can be established. In this case, the dean of the faculty appoints a committee consisting of members of several departments. Such a committee has all the academic powers of a regular department and administers appropriate programs.

It is possible to go even further. The president of the university, who has not yet been mentioned, can appoint committees that consist of members of different faculties to administer inter-faculty programs such as the history of education (the faculty of education joining with the department of history, which is part of the faculty of arts and sciences), or the history and philosophy of religion (the faculty of divinity and the departments of history and of philosophy, which are part of the faculty of arts and sciences), or medical sciences (the faculty of medicine and the departments of chemistry and biology, which are part of the faculty of arts and sciences). Incidentally, the dependence of most interdisciplinary programs on subjects taught by a faculty of arts and sciences emphasizes the basic role of that faculty in a well-organized university.

It must be obvious that there are many demands on an American professor's time in addition to those of teaching and research. Thus the relatively large amount of committee work expected of American faculty members is part of the price of democracy. Moreover, the many letters of recommendation that professors are asked to write on behalf of applicants for scholarships and fellowships are part of the price of an extensive system of financial aid for students. On the other hand, the American professor is spared the chore of examining students in secondary schools.

The central administration of an American university consists normally of a president (who may occasionally be known as rector or chancellor) and a board of trustees. The president of the university, who is selected and named by the trustees and may even preside over their meetings as well as over meetings of his university's several faculties, may be a professor, or a man active in politics, or a highly respected citizen with no political or academic affiliation. A legitimate question might well be: how does it happen that the president of a great American university is not himself an academic person? The answer suggests one of the principal activities of the president: he must take care of the finances of his institution. He must supervise his university's relations with its alumni, with business and industry, with the great philanthropic foundations, and with government — federal, state, and local. He must be a person who is capable of representing his university in a type of negotiation that the majority of professors prefer to leave to more practical men. Because of their complex and specialized functions the presidents of American universities normally stay in office for a long period of years. The position does not rotate as does the vice-chancellorship of major English universities.

The board of trustees may in its entirety act as the direct controlling body of the institution, or may be subdivided, a small group of individuals actually exercising the authority, subject to ratification by the remaining members. Many American universities, in particular the private universities, are, from the legal point of view, nonprofit corporations operating under state charter. The board of trustees thus represents the legally constituted authority of the university. It owns the property of the university. It names the president and confirms the appointment of the faculty members and administrative officials. It rarely exercises any purely educational authority, since the faculties are held to be autonomous in this respect. The board of trustees, or regents, or overseers, as they are occasionally called, is generally composed of persons who are not part of the academic world, but are, rather, lawyers or doctors or businessmen. In some universities, the board members are elected by the former students, the alumni. In others they are named by the state government. At times the members name their own successors.

In general, relations between the president and the board of trustees on the one hand and the faculties on the other are excellent. The trustees are men or women of breadth of vision and of good will. They are educated. They realize what an important role they have in our modern society and act responsibly. At times, of course, pressures can develop. For example, the governing board of a private university might become dominated by a group of businessmen of a given economic philosophy, or the trustees of a state or municipal university might be influenced by a group of politicians. Such occurrences are relatively infrequent, and the central university administration rarely takes steps to jeopardize the precious academic freedom that is the direct result of the system of life tenure which the professors enjoy. Yet there have been some rather notable examples of interference with academic freedom in the past, particularly on the part of state authorities. If such interference develops in one university, there is an almost instantaneous reaction throughout the entire American university world, and usually a solution favorable to the professors is found.

The administrative functions of the several schools and colleges that comprise an American university may be performed independently within the framework of these schools and colleges, or they may be performed by central university offices, often housed in a large, impressive administration building. In the latter case there is one admissions office and one registrar for the entire university.

The administration of an American university has been described and no mention made of the students! With few exceptions, as already stated, they have no voice in administrative matters.

The university exists; the faculty sets the curriculum, with great freedom of choice, to be sure. The students accept, or do not accept. If they do not accept, they go to another university, a not infrequent occurrence. In some institutions, especially in the liberal-arts colleges, the students elect a student council to represent them vis-à-vis the administration. The deans and the department chairmen respect the advice of the students, read their reports, and occasionally adopt their ideas. It is true, on the other hand, that in some colleges the students have a real voice in the government of their school. Moreover, students in not a few institutions conduct surveys in order to evaluate their courses and their teachers.

The formal role of the student in university administration is thus purely advisory and consultative. American students do not have, and do not seek, a direct voice in university government. They do have a powerful indirect voice, however, for the tradition of freedom of choice of courses to follow allows the students to express their sentiments not only for or against individual professors but even concerning whole departments or programs of study.

If the enrolled students have but a small voice within the university organization, the former students, that is, the graduates or alumni, are extremely influential. The explanation is simple: the alumni contribute money, large sums of money. Since they contribute money, they wish to have a voice in how it is spent. An American university does not like to operate in a vacuum and frankly esteems highly the opinions and the suggestions of the alumni. As a result, a very amicable relation exists between the university and its graduates. The university publishes a bulletin dedicated to the alumni; the latter subscribe to it. The university organizes national campaigns to raise money; the alumni respond with remarkable generosity. In the chapter on the financing of higher education more details are given.

In addition to the central core of the university, there is a whole series of auxiliary services. One of these is the construction and maintenance of buildings. This is an enormous task, requiring a separate and highly specialized department, almost a ministry, called the department of buildings and grounds. In my opinion, American colleges and universities have spent far too much money constructing beautiful buildings and cutting enormous and velvety lawns, lawns that are esthetically pleasing but of little educational value. Money is indispensable for faculty salaries, books, laboratories, and scholarships. If there is money to spare, all well and good: luxurious buildings and verdant lawns. Unfortunately, I do not know of a single American university that has enough money for its primary needs.

There are also extensive university medical services, which care for both the physical and the mental health of the students. The medical services are constantly increasing in scope — and cost — and thought is at long last being given to the university's responsibility for the physical and mental health of its faculty.

There are other auxiliary services in the organization of an American university. They usually belong, however, not to the central administration, but to a particular college or graduate school. There is usually a vocational guidance center, to assist the student in selecting a degree program in harmony with his interests and aptitude. Closely related to this center is the placement bureau, which seeks to find suitable employment for the graduates. Then there may be a central testing service, which is involved in various and sundry aptitude, achievement, and placement tests. Lastly, there may be a study-counsel center, which assists the student, often for a nominal fee, in his study habits, attempts to improve his rate of reading, and furnishes extra help in specific academic courses. A center of the latter type performs an additional, albeit negative function: by its very existence under official university auspices it impedes the development of commercially oriented tutorial schools and other agencies which aim to assist the student to the detriment of his education.

Mention must be made of athletics, in view of the importance of this subject in American movies. Athletics, teams, the great interuniversity games, are almost exclusively at the undergraduate level and are a part of student life in the liberal-arts colleges. Football, the most widely publicized college and university sport, presents many financial problems, and some educators have questioned the wisdom of supporting it on the traditional lavish scale. A football program is costly to run, and fluctuation in the quality of teams over the years makes gate receipts uncertain. When teams are victorious and receipts high, football contributes to the physical development not only of the participants but also of the entire student body, for the income from it helps defray the cost of the total athletic and physical exercise program.

There are two other activities in the majority of large American universities that are of great importance in bearing witness to the interest of these universities in adult education. They are summer schools and university extension programs.

Although some universities operate the year round on a four-quarter system, the normal American academic year runs from the end of September until the beginning or middle of June. July and August are thus left entirely free for a different type of academic activity. During these two months there are the summer schools, which permit regular students to make up deficiencies or accelerate the attainment of their degree and also permit practicing teachers to acquire more knowledge of their subject matter or of pedagogic techniques. Some summer schools last six weeks, others eight weeks. Occasionally, a university runs two successive six-week summer sessions. In several parts of the United States there are university summer schools that specialize in the teaching of English to foreigners.

What is called university extension is the teaching, normally done at night or in the late afternoon or on Saturday morning, that is specially arranged for adults who work during the day. This teaching is a very important service which the universities perform for their local communities, and men and women in large numbers take advantage of it. The universities even confer degrees on extension students, for instance, that of Adjunct in Arts. Adult education, which ranges from courses in pottery-making to high-level courses in the humanities, is assuming ever greater proportions, and television is being utilized to advantage. It is to be expected that adult education will become a more integral part of formal studies, for it is now realized that learning is a process that continues throughout life and is not confined to childhood and adolescence. Moreover, university teachers often find that considerable personal satisfaction is to be derived from teaching mature and responsive adults who are motivated by a genuine love of learning and not by the requirements of a degree.

In order that the relation between the purely academic aspect and the various services within the organization of at least one American university may by appreciated, it may be of interest to cite some statistics concerning Harvard University. For the academic year 1958–1959, the total expenses amounted to approximately $66,000,000. Of this sum, about $17,500,000 was paid as salaries to the teaching staff and academic persons in general. About $18,300,000 went as salaries to employees. During that year there were about 4,300 paid members of the teaching staff, including administrative officers and part-time and apprentice teachers. There were about 4,600 regular employees and a large number of temporary or so-called casual employees. The total student enrollment for the year was over 11,000 men and women. In addition, Harvard faculties provided instruction for almost 1,800 women registered in Radcliffe College, a separate corporation associated with Harvard University.

III

Student Life in American Colleges and Universities

HOLLYWOOD MOVIES have already given the world an idea of student life in American colleges and universities. Whatever this idea may be, student life in all of our colleges is at times very pleasant, and in some of our colleges it is always very pleasant. The professors often wonder how the students ever find any time for their studies.

This chapter is concerned almost exclusively with student life in the colleges of liberal arts, the four-year colleges, independent or university, which prepare for the degree of Bachelor of Arts or Bachelor of Science. Unfortunately, the poor graduate students usually have to study long hours and must be satisfied with the glorious memory of what they did as undergraduates. Yet, graduate-student life is changing, is acquiring some of the more human aspects of college life; mention of these changes will be made at the end of the chapter.

The present-day student life that is so characteristic of American colleges did not evolve purely by chance. It is the natural result of an educational philosophy that has existed for many years. Americans want the college education of their students, both male and female, to be complete, all-inclusive. "The education of the whole man" is their phrase. They want to cultivate the physical and social and moral aspects of the student's life as well as the intellectual and esthetic. Therefore they have established an extensive system of athletics and physical exercise. They have built great religious centers, and also large dormitories with common rooms, dining halls, game rooms, music-practice rooms, and photographic dark rooms. They encourage a whole series of so-called "extracurricular" activities such as dramatic clubs, debating societies, student newspapers, literary reviews, humor magazines, and political clubs and forums.

In order for the student to derive the maximum profit from all that is offered him in college, he must be "in residence," that is, must live in a college dormitory, eat in a college dining hall, and devote almost his entire life during the academic year to the college curriculum in its broadest sense. Consequently, the following description is limited to colleges that are residential, where the students live at or near the college, and not at home. The two types of college exist. Some of the municipal colleges are exclusively academic institutions; the students go to class and use the library and that is all. They live with their parents or in a hired room in the city or town, but away from the college. The other colleges are complete communities in miniature, and in general are located in small cities or towns, which come to be dominated by the colleges, often to the accompaniment of a certain amount of friction between "town and gown."

In a residential college the student lives in a dormitory, sometimes in a single room alone, more generally with one or more roommates. Usually these roommates are strangers. They are assigned by the college administration with the idea of habituating the student to a communal type of life. For the same reason the student takes his meals in a dining hall and, in the process, learns to converse with students, and occasionally faculty members, who have other interests and other opinions.

In some universities, especially in the larger ones, the dormitories and dining halls are enormous and rather impersonal. In others, there is a slightly different system, an adaptation of the English college system. Thus at Harvard there are eight "houses," that is, dormitories, but more than dormitories.

Each house, or as Yale University calls them, "college," is a complete community. It houses some 300 to 400 students and has a dining hall, common rooms, and library of its own, and even a group of professors who form the house staff, a tiny faculty. The purpose of these houses is twofold: to place the student in direct and immediate contact with a portion of the faculty, a most necessary purpose in view of the size and impersonality of the university and the difficulty students have in becoming acquainted with faculty members, and to furnish an opportunity for the students to know each other intimately and to exchange ideas outside of class. Each house is directed by a master, who is an experienced professor with a strong personal interest in the education of youth. It should be pointed out that the house system is not usual in the United States, for a very good reason: it costs a great deal of money.

An undergraduate college such as Harvard's, although primarily residential, inevitably has a sizeable proportion of commuters who live within easy distance of the university. For them a commuters' center is provided, a "house" in all respects but for living quarters.

In a large number of American colleges and universities there are many fraternities and sororities, which are really independent private clubs with selective admission for men and women, respectively. These organizations, which are often local chapters of national fraternities or sororities, usually own their own buildings, which serve as social centers and in which many of the members have their living accommodations and take their meals.

Before discussing college studies, a word concerning the education of women. When women first began attending colleges, they went as a general rule to colleges that admitted only members of their own sex. This tradition still continues, and many well-known liberal-arts colleges are for one sex only — Bryn Mawr, Mills, Mount Holyoke, Smith, Sweet Briar, Vassar, Wellesley for women; Amherst, Bowdoin, Dartmouth, Kenyon, Williams for men. With the success of the feminist movement in the United States, and with widespread acceptance of the idea of the equality of the sexes, colleges and even universities were founded for both sexes, coeducational institutions, as they are called, the female students being known as coeds. Thus the great state and municipal universities are for both men and women.

As for the heart of student life, the students normally take four or five courses a term, for two terms (or semesters) a year, for four years. They have a wide choice of fields of specialization and usually a fairly broad choice of courses within their fields. They almost always have a wide selection of "electives," that is, courses they are free to elect or choose outside their fields of specialization. As a general rule each course meets three times a week, each meeting lasting fifty minutes. In many institutions the courses are calculated in terms of credit hours or semester hours; a course meeting three hours a week for one semester is evaluated at three credits or points, 120 such credits being required for the bachelor's degree. The students are expected to study two hours out of class for each fifty-minute period in class. Thus, theoretically, they devote from thirty-five to forty hours a week to their studies, more if any of their courses include long laboratory periods. Each term lasts about fifteen weeks. There are two weeks of vacation for Christmas and one week at Easter or early in April.

The courses or credits that a student accumulates toward an academic degree at one university may be transferred to another university if the latter admits the student concerned. When so admitted, the student is called a transfer-student and is said to be admitted to advanced standing. As there is little formal interuniversity organization in the United States there is no automatic process whereby a student may apply one university's credits to another university's degree. The individual universities are free to use their own judgment in accepting transfer-students. The better universities are anxious to uphold the reputation of their degrees. They are therefore reluctant to accept credits earned at what they consider to be inferior institutions, for, although the degrees of all universities are theoretically equally valid, there is in fact a subtle scale of prestige that operates to characterize and categorize universities and their degrees. Consequently, the degrees of some institutions mean far more in the popular mind than those of other institutions. The distinction very often reflects real difference in the quality of the institutions compared.

In the United States there are, in general, two types of course. One is the universal, the medieval. It often consists of a series of lectures delivered by the master to an audience of possibly 500 students, who sleep, watch the clock, knit, write each other notes, read the newspaper, and at times listen to the professor and take notes. The professor reads his lectures, perhaps for the twentieth time. There is little exchange of ideas between teacher and student. American students are beginning to express their opposition to this type of instruction, and with very good results.

The other type of course is given to a small class, of from fifteen to thirty students, with considerable discussion, usually based on previously assigned reading, the class often ending up in a local restaurant over a cup of coffee or a "coke." Unfortunately, just as in the case of the house system, small classes are very costly and can usually be provided only for advanced undergraduates, in which case they are often called seminars and are modeled after the graduate-student seminars. A compromise is therefore effected: the professor delivers his lectures once or twice a week to all the students in the course, and for the remaining meetings the students are divided into small groups each under the direction of a younger teacher. If the college is part of a university, these small groups, or sections, are often taught by graduate students.

A grave defect of higher education in the United States, especially in the liberal-arts colleges, is the concept of the individual course as the basic ingredient of education. Taking courses seems to be more important than acquiring knowledge. Courses have become in many instances self-contained packaged units, complete with syllabus, carefully prepared lectures, well considered assigned reading, and examinations. College graduates, in referring back to their college education, often state that they "took psychology" (or some other subject), meaning they took a course in it, rather than that they "studied psychology" or "learned psychology." They are probably being honest, for taking a course is no guarantee that knowledge is acquired. A good course, however, may aid in the acquisition of both knowledge and wisdom.

As in all aspects of higher education in the United States, there is an enormous variation in instructional practices throughout the country, and there is constant experimentation. Indeed, in recent years the "case method," formerly used almost exclusively in law schools, has been introduced on a small scale in the colleges. For many years practical exercises in the laboratory have been an integral part of instruction in the natural sciences. As a result, American institutions of higher education have built large and costly instructional laboratories for the use of students. They are quite independent of, although often in the same building as, the research laboratories of the faculty and advanced graduate students. As for subjects like geology, the inclusion of field trips as part of the instruction is standard practice. At the present time many institutions are installing language laboratories, rooms equipped with from thirty to one hundred tape-recorders to permit students of foreign languages to acquire aural-oral training during the study hours outside of class.

In the independent college the teachers know the students, classes are small, and the students derive considerable profit from the close contact with the faculty. On the other hand, the majority of the independent colleges do not have sufficient funds to hire the great names in the academic profession, who prefer to teach in the universities, where they can conduct research and have graduate students. Thus there are advantages on both sides. Some students, or their fathers, prefer the independent college, others the university college.

In the United States the students, or their parents, have an absolutely free choice as to the type of institution to attend, public or private, independent college or university college, church-related or non-church-related. No future employer, governmental or private, will require that the degree be from a certain type of institution. Inasmuch as there is no federal control of education, no Ministry of Education, and relatively little control by the states, there is no legal or employment advantage to be derived from attending a public institution, which, although "public," is not in any sense "official." As will be seen in a later chapter, professional licensing is independent both of the universities and of the federal government; it is a function of the state.

In the United States students and faculty alike are afflicted by written examinations. At the end of each semester in each course there is usually a final written examination of two or three hours' duration. Often there is a one-hour examination in the middle of the course. In some colleges there are in addition general examinations covering the whole field of specialization at the end of the third or fourth year. As examinations are often written in little blank books with blue covers, the term "blue-book" has become closely identified with examination. As a rule, the marks given in examinations, and as final grades in courses, are numbers or letters. The numbers are percentages, 100 per cent being the highest mark possible. Of the letters, A means between 90 and 100 per cent; B, between 80 and 90; C, 70 to 80; D, 60 to 70; and E, below 60. Generally, 60 is the critical mark; below 60 means that the examination or the course is not satisfactorily passed and must be repeated or replaced by an additional course. A mark between 60 and 70, that is, D, is not satisfactory, but repetition or replacement is not required.

On occasion the general public becomes aroused about alleged cheating in college examinations. It is undeniable that some cheating exists, although the practice is by no means so extensive as to require adoption of oral examinations in lieu of the traditional written examinations.

In many colleges the baccalaureate is awarded with various degrees of honors, *summa cum laude, magna cum laude, cum laude,* or no honors. The basis for determining the honors is often simply the grades the student received during his four years. In other colleges the students must announce their candidacy for honors and do extra work, that is, take extra courses within their field of concentration ("major") and, in some fields, write a thesis of perhaps 10,000 words.

Another type of highly coveted honor in American colleges and universities is election to membership in one or more of the several honor societies. A large number of these societies are designated by Greek letters; they are national, with many local chapters. The best known is Phi Beta Kappa, which was organized in 1776 and came to be limited to the field of liberal arts. Other honor societies of broad scope are Tau Beta Pi (engineering), Sigma Xi (scientific research), Delta Epsilon Sigma (Catholic colleges and universities), and Phi Kappa Phi (all fields).

In the American educational system the rank or class standing of the student (for example, number 14 out of 159) in general does not have the significance that it does in other educational systems and is often not calculated.

Occasionally, candidates for honors are, during their last years in college, assigned to a tutor, a member of the teaching staff with whom they work individually. As the tutorial system is very expensive, an alternate method of instruction may be the preceptorial system, in which the preceptor meets the students in small groups of five or six, rather than individually. The friendship begun in college between student and tutor or preceptor is often very lasting; even while in college the teacher occasionally invites the student to his home for tea or dinner, and, if unmarried, is invited by the student to the latter's home for vacation periods.

The academic year closes with "commencement," the round of ceremonies in the course of which degrees are formally conferred by the university on those who are "graduating" and are about to commence life. The degree candidates wear the traditional cap and gown, a costume that is less and less used at other times during the year as institutions become larger and larger.

Sleeping, eating, and forty hours of study amount to a maximum of 117 hours per week. Fifty-one remain to be accounted for. Movies and television take their share. There are dances and "dates." There are public lectures in the late afternoon or after dinner, and concerts. There are dramatic productions, put on either by students or by professional troupes. There are club meetings of every conceivable type. There are sports.

In many American universities there is a large well-equipped building that serves as a center for almost all the student extracurricular activities. It is called a student center or "union," and has public lounges, a theater, offices for clubs, cafeteria, soda bar, swimming pool, and bedrooms for guests.

Men students in most colleges have complete personal freedom; they can come and go as they wish during the day or night. Women students have some restrictions. Thus, as an example, first-year women students, or "freshmen," might not be allowed out of the dormitory after ten o'clock in the evening except for special occasions, such as dances, when they must return by one o'clock. During the other three years, that is, as sophomores, juniors, or seniors, the women have fewer restrictions. It is true that in some men's colleges there are similar rules, but these colleges are the exception.

As for sports, which play a large part in college life, the movies depict only the outstanding games between university teams, with eleven athletes representing a student body of perhaps 5,000. There are actually many more teams, especially teams representing clubs or dormitories, which participate in intramural competitions.

In these various ways the students spend four years. For many it is an ideal life. Until their death they retain a sentimental attachment to their alma mater, or fostering mother, as Americans aptly call it. They teach their children the many college songs they sang at athletic contests and social events, and when they are older and are earning substantial salaries they demonstrate their loyalty and gratitude by making large financial contributions.

For some students, life is more difficult because they are poor and have to earn money by working. College expenses are often very high. For example, in a private residential college they may amount to $2,500 or $2,800 per academic year. In a state or municipal college, the expenses are less, but even so they are at least $800. Obviously if a student lives and eats at home, a college education costs much less. The figures quoted include tuition, fees, room, meals, books, and personal expenses; they do not include travel between home and college. There are numerous scholarships and fellowships for the poorer students. Yet these funds are sufficient for paying only a part of the expenses of a minority of the students, and, moreover, they are usually reserved for students of exceptional intellectual, or perhaps in the case of some colleges, athletic ability. And so a part of the student body works during the academic year, two hours a day, perhaps five or six, maybe even all night. Students wait on table in the dining halls, work in libraries, and tutor backward but more wealthy colleagues. If a student works in order to earn money, there is often an educational loss. In order to get the most out of college, the student must devote all his waking hours to it. On the other hand, some colleges, notably Antioch College in the State of Ohio, have evolved work-study plans in which remunerative employment is an integral part of the program.

Working one's way through college is a method of acquiring a college education for the student who has neither the necessary intellectual capacity to qualify for a scholarship or fellowship nor the parents fortunate enough to have the necessary money ready at hand. Because of the obvious disadvantages of working while studying, other means of financing students are employed. One involves loan funds. Many institutions have large loan funds and encourage students to borrow by not charging interest while they are still studying and charging only a small rate of interest pending repayment after graduation. It should be added that these loan funds are normally not available to students from abroad, who may usually borrow no more than a small amount for a short period of time (less than a year).

Individual states have authorized the setting up of what are referred to as nonprofit "higher education assistance corporations." Through the agency of such an organization in his home state, a student can borrow sizeable sums of money to be used at the college or university of his choice, regardless of the state in which it is located, and to be paid back after he terminates his studies.

As a former dean of a graduate school of arts and sciences who is thoroughly familiar with all the finanical pressures that accompany marriage, the setting up of a home, and the raising of children, I feel constrained to state that I view with alarm these trends in the direction of encouraging students to borrow money. In my opinion they are not destined to be of real long-term assistance to young men and women but rather to tie a mill-stone around their necks.

A variation of the loan scheme has been in effect since 1938. Called The Tuition Plan, it came about as a result of a college and university practice that requires advance payment of tuition and other charges. Under this plan the parents can pay monthly for the education of their offspring, while the institution receives its fees in full before the beginning of each term.

In order to solve the problem of the high cost of a college education and also to take care of students who are not interested in spending four years away from home, a new type of two-year community college is gaining favor in the United States. Such colleges award a degree of Associate in Arts. In at least one state the community college is integrated into the public-school system and is part of what is known as the 6–4–4 plan (six years of elementary school, four years of secondary school, and four years of community college). This pattern contrasts with the widespread 6–3–3 plan (six years of elementary school, three years of junior high school, and three years of high school) and with the older 4–4–4 plan (four years of "primary" school, four years of "grammar" school, and four years of high school). On the other hand, in at least one other state the community college is part of the system of higher education. The expression "junior college," which used to designate a private two-year college, is now being changed in some cases to the one word "college" in order to avoid misunderstanding of its purpose and function.

At the beginning of this chapter, reference was made to graduate-student life. In general, medical schools, law schools, graduate schools of arts and sciences, and others are adopting many of the activities formerly peculiar to the undergraduate colleges. New graduate-student centers, with comfortable living accommodations and good dining halls, have been built, and more attention is being paid to the physical and, even more important, the mental health of the advanced students. Of course, graduate students are more apt to be married than undergraduates, and consequently tend to have less interest in the com-

munity life. Yet even married students and their families are not neglected by the university officials, who often provide housing for them, arrange social programs for their wives, and, since World War II at least, operate nursery schools for their children.

What conclusions may be drawn from this description of student life in American colleges and universities? Perhaps the impression has been given that it is too perfect. Actually, it can be severely criticized. In general it can be concluded that Americans spoil their college students. The college years for many students are too easy, too artificial. The philosophy that underlies the undergraduate program presupposes that the students are being prepared for life. One cannot be sure. Yet the fact is that the four college years are for many Americans the period of transition between adolescence and adulthood. Americans often learn the social amenities in college; they learn to drink and to know the opposite sex. They are away from home and they become independent. Many parents and educational theorists believe that, if college facilitates this transition, it is playing an important and useful role.

IV

Curriculum Problems in American Liberal-Arts Colleges

In this chapter a few of the outstanding curriculum problems of American colleges are discussed in some detail. In general it may be said that the requirements for the degrees of Bachelor of Arts and Bachelor of Science are approximately the same throughout the United States; one college introduces

an innovation and sooner or later most of the others copy it. There are no legal reasons why this is so, no regulations of the state or federal governments that require uniformity of curriculum. Perhaps the greatest force operating toward uniformity is the existence of admission requirements, explicit or implied, on the part of graduate schools. That college is very courageous which strikes out, as the University of Chicago has done, in a substantially new direction. Even church colleges, including the Catholic colleges, conform in general to the secular pattern, although they require courses in, for example, church history, philosophy, and doctrine, over and above other subjects, and strive to create a total religious environment for the students.

The outstanding curriculum problem is the preservation of an equilibrium between specialization, preprofessional preparation, on the one hand, and general education, preparation for life and citizenship, on the other. This problem is far from being solved. In the following description of some of the aspects of this problem, several references will be made to Harvard University, which has long endeavored to reach a solution.

The evolution of the liberal-arts curriculum is very significant, so a little Harvard history may be in order. From the seventeenth to the middle of the nineteenth century the curriculum in Harvard College was fixed, rigid, classical. From this extreme the college went directly to the other. President Charles William Eliot (in office from 1869 to 1909) introduced the free-elective system; the students could study what they wished. The new system was the natural and inevitable product of the German specialization which was introduced into the United States about that time. The professors taught specialized courses and wanted students. Consequently, the students had complete liberty in the selection of their courses, and the ensemble of those they took during the required four years was often more than a little ridiculous.

The third phase in the evolution of the curriculum began under the presidency of Abbott Lawrence Lowell, who succeeded President Eliot in 1909. President Lowell introduced an entirely different system, known as concentration and distribution. Each student was required to follow a program of specialization, to concentrate, during the four years, or at least during the sophomore, junior, and senior years. Of the sixteen full-year courses required for the bachelor's degree, six, seven, on occasion eight, had to be within the field of concentration. There was free choice as far as the field of concentration was concerned. Within the field selected, however, the program was more or less fixed. For a supposedly liberal-arts college such a system could have been very undesirable, with an untoward emphasis on specialization. President Lowell and his colleagues realized this and included a program of distribution alongside the system of concentration. Thus, several of the remaining courses required for the degree, at least five out of sixteen, had to be distributed among subjects unrelated to the field of concentration. For example, each student was obliged to take a course in English composition, a course in natural science, one in social science, one in either mathematics or philosophy, and one in literature. As a result, the breadth of the individual's education was to some extent assured, regardless of the field of specialization.

Harvard College still has the system of concentration. The system of distribution was modified immediately after World War II because it allegedly had the following important defect. The rules stipulated that students were required to take courses in, let us say, natural science. There was a choice among elementary physics, elementary chemistry, and elementary biology.

There were more advanced courses for students who had studied one of these subjects in high school and wished to continue it. The student specializing in a subject from among the humanities would take a course in an elementary science to satisfy the requirement. Unfortunately, the course would be taught not from the point of view, and in the interest, of the student of the humanities, or at least so it is argued by the defenders of "general education," but rather from the point of view of a future concentrator in that science. It would be taught by scientists for scientists. It would not present the broad problems of the science, the general scientific method, the impact of science in general on modern society, the resulting social problems, and so on. It would present essential subdivisions as basic subjects for students who were going on in the specific science. In short, the individual's broad general education suffered.

For that reason, in early 1949, the Faculty of Arts and Sciences, under the presidency of Dr. James Bryant Conant, who succeeded President Lowell in 1933 and presided over Harvard until 1953, adopted a new system of distribution called "general education." There are now much the same regulations as before, except that the faculty offers more general courses, nonspecialized courses that are designed to contribute to the student's general intellectual training. Thus, within the humanities the freshman during 1959–60 can choose among five courses: Crisis and the Individual in Drama and History and in Biography and Fiction; Ideas of Man and the World in Western Thought; Introduction to Literature; Uses of the Comic Spirit; and The Experience of the Drama. In the social sciences there are six courses: Introduc-

tion to the Development of Western Civilization; Western Thought and Institutions; Natural Man and Ideal Man in Western Thought; Ideas and Social Change in European History; Freedom and Authority in the Modern World; and The Role of Law in Anglo-American History. In the natural sciences there are also six courses: Foundations of Modern Physical Science; Historical Introduction to the Physical Sciences; The Enterprise of Science; Principles and Problems of the Biological Sciences; Light, the Atom and the Stars; and The Earth — Past and Present.

Harvard is not the only institution, nor even the first, to have introduced general education. Columbia University has long included general-education courses in the curriculum of its liberal-arts college, Columbia College. Programs not unlike general education but known by other names have also been in existence for a number of years, as, for example, the "great books" programs of St. John's College in Annapolis, Maryland, and of the University of Chicago.

The success of the system of general education in American colleges depends on the interest of the faculties concerned. If a teaching staff composed essentially of specialists wishes to give courses of a general nature, success is guaranteed. On the other hand, the very success of a general education program may carry in its wake a new and serious problem — a diminishing cultivation of exotic subjects that are not appropriate for undergraduate concentration and do not fit directly into a general education program. If universities neglect these subjects, they fail in a most important part of their mission. A striking example of such failure is furnished by unusual language fields.

The Congress regarded certain lacunae in university offerings as so serious that, in the National Defense Education Act of 1958 it specifically provided for the encouragement of study of Arabic, Chinese, Hindi, Japanese, Portuguese, and Russian.

The attitude of the specialized faculty is likewise important in the system of concentration. Theoretically, American colleges require specialization for educational and not for practical reasons. They believe that to know one subject thoroughly is to learn the nature of knowledge, the difficulty of arriving at truth. Thus the program of concentration in a given subject should be so organized as to employ this subject as an exemplification of the nature of knowledge in the broadest sense.

Lest the impression be given that overspecialization is a universal defect in American higher education, it should in all fairness be pointed out that in some of the smaller liberal-arts colleges there is too much general education and too little specialization, too little of the discipline that is a by-product of concentration. The explanation is quite simple. These institutions have small faculties; the individual teachers must often give instruction in more than one subject and are generally so occupied that they have no time to over-specialize. Such colleges are endeavoring to improve their programs by requiring more specialization and integration of the subjects studied.

The reader may well be puzzled at the rather low level of the college education of American youth. The students are from eighteen to twenty-one years of age. They have already completed at least twelve years of prior schooling. What did they learn before entering college? From the traditional academic point of view, they perhaps learned very

little. This conclusion is by no means a condemnation of American elementary and secondary schools but rather is an indication of the many changes that have taken place in recent years in the American school system. In times past, the colleges required their students to have studied certain subjects prior to being admitted to college. Thus they may have required four years of Latin, three years of English, three years of mathematics, a year of science, two years of history, and two or three years of a modern foreign language. The system of definitely announced prerequisites for admission was a good one for that period.

Social and economic conditions, however, have changed considerably in the United States since 1933, the beginning of the presidencies of Dr. Conant — and of Mr. Roosevelt. The secondary schools, especially the municipal high schools, have had to modify their curriculum in order to satisfy the needs of the many students who, alas, do not even now go on to college in spite of the general American philosophy of equal educational opportunity. When this modification in the secondary-school curriculum occurred, the colleges could well have continued to require certain preparatory subjects. In this case only the graduates of a few private preparatory schools and of a very few classical high schools would have been admitted. The composition of the college student body would have been very homogeneous but in no way representative of the youth of the nation. What the colleges in fact did was to modify the entrance requirements. They now want to be assured that the students whom they admit have an aptitude for the college program; the knowledge that they possess is, according to this educational theory, of lesser importance. The pendulum is now swinging back, however. Elementary and secondary schools are constantly being improved, as for example in the teaching of mathematics, science, and foreign languages. It is possible that colleges will once again be able to require training in specific subjects as a prerequisite for admission.

The use of so-called aptitude tests has greatly increased in recent years. They are very important in the selection of students for both undergraduate and graduate schools as well as in vocational guidance. Alongside the aptitude tests there is a series of placement tests, which aid the faculty members in advising the students which courses they are best prepared to take. These latter tests are an inevitable consequence of the admissions system. Thus, in the case of the French language, students come to college with one, two, three, four or more years of the language, or none at all. The quality of secondary-school teaching varies considerably; two years of French in one school might well be the equivalent of four years in another. College teachers require more precise information concerning their new students than that furnished by the transcripts of their secondary-school studies. Hence, the placement tests, which now, because of the extensive development of tape-recorders, can cover aural-oral as well as written work.

A second great problem at the American undergraduate level is the education of women. This is not the place to go into the history of the feminist movement in the United States. The educational result of the movement was that the education of men and women became identical, perhaps because many American men desire a wife who is an intellectual companion as well as a cook and a mother of their children. The curriculum of the women's colleges is different in only a very few respects from that of the men's colleges. In coeducational institutions all the students take the same courses, men and women together. There are, of course, women's home economics and secretarial colleges; when their programs are of four years' duration, liberal-arts subjects are included. Paradoxically enough, it is probably accurate to say that, when men and women follow the same bachelor's program in an American liberal-arts college, the women often derive considerably more benefit, and for a simple reason: they are less preoccupied with specialization and professional preparation, with the concomitant emphasis on grades, than are the men, and consequently they are prepared to take from their courses the best that they have to offer.

The desirability of having an identical curriculum for men and women is now questioned. Perhaps curriculum committees, especially those in coeducational institutions, have not given sufficient thought to the very real differences betwen the sexes, differences that might demand dissimilarities in the treatment of subject matter, if not in the subject matter itself. On the other hand, there is the view that students of both sexes should follow the same curriculum, which, in its turn, should be appropriate for both. This view seems to be supported by those men students who believe that, if there are to be courses in child psychology, marriage, and human relations, they should take them, too.

A third problem, which can only be alluded to here, is the role of the teaching of the creative arts, writing, painting, musical composition, dramatic production, even radio and television programing and movie production, in an American university. Conservative opinion has so far rejected the inclusion of many of these subjects in the liberal-arts programs. Yet much use is made of creative work in the elementary schools. Perhaps the experimentation which has been done in some of the far-seeing colleges may become more generally accepted.

A fourth and very widely discussed problem concerning the curriculum in American liberal-arts colleges is the place of foreign langauges in the program, that is, the faculty requirements to the effect that every student, regardless of his personal interests, must study at least one language not his native tongue.

In the past, "educated" Americans studied Latin for four or five years and French for three or more years in secondary school, and then took two or three years more of French and perhaps a year or two of German in college. Today Americans study foreign languages much less, or, more precisely, more Americans study fewer languages because more Americans go to college. Here is the key to the problem. There are millions of students in American high schools and colleges. Not all of them can be required to study languages, for not all of them are going to need languages later in life. Therefore, the present practice is the requirement that the student know one language at least superficially before he receives the bachelor's degree. Obviously there are many courses in foreign languages and large numbers of students take them. Yet the requirement to take them, as part of the educational philosophy, seems to be less widespread than formerly. On the other hand, a widely publicized effort by the Modern Language Association during the past

few years has aroused public opinion concerning language learning. Not only have some liberal-arts colleges restored degree language requirements, but there has also been a widespread and successful effort to introduce the teaching of foreign languages in the elementary schools.

If American students are obliged to study a foreign langauge, what languages are acceptable? Formerly they were Latin, Greek, French, German, possibly Italian, in other words, the languages that were considered to have the greatest cultural value, the genteel languages. Today there is a tendency to include any language in the world. From the point of view of educational policy all languages are acceptable not only because there is today only one world, with international problems of pressing importance, but also because the study of any foreign language gives the student those educational values that are deemed of importance: an acquaintance with how other peoples think, poetic values, a better acquaintance with the student's own language. These values are all debatable, and it is perhaps true that insistence on them rather than on practical results, such as the ability simply to handle foreign languages, has led to the weakening of foreign-language requirements.

If the students are obliged to study a foreign language, must they acquire a reading knowledge, a speaking knowledge, or both? For many years, and in particular since World War II, this phase of the language-teaching problem has been of concern to about every liberal-arts faculty in the United States. It must be remembered that the American system of higher education is vast. The curriculum is designed for all students, not just for the few, the privileged, those who are going to enter a ministry of foreign affairs. The answer to the question is not easy. In many colleges it is believed that the foreign-language requirement should be, above all else, in terms of reading, it being fully recognized that a speaking ability is a necessary prerequisite to the attainment of a true reading knowledge.

A fifth curriculum problem concerns the proper use of audio-visual aids. The last few years have witnessed an enormous development of such devices, which are being very effectively used, for example, to supplement classroom language teaching. Most promising results seem to be offered by experimentation with so-called "closed-circuit" television, self-contained within and confined to the walls of a single institution. The increase in the use of audio-visual aids has opened up the possibility of a complete re-evaluation of the use of highly qualified and trained personnel in college and university teaching. By the proper use of machines such personnel may more easily reach large audiences and so bring about a situation in which they can earn salaries more nearly commensurate than at present with their contributions to society.

Another problem of increasing concern not only to American educators but to responsible members of the community at large is the proper place of religion in the curriculum of the secular, or "non-denominational," or "non-church-related" undergraduate college. Many students feel that a spiritual void in the curriculum needs to be filled, and many parents and churchmen agree with them. Many teachers in the secular colleges feel that a serious omission occurs when consideration of religion and religious values is left out of the curriculum. Many serious scholars feel that their company is not complete without representation from theology.

On the other hand, in a country like the United States in which there is no state religion and in which the various religions live in more or less complete harmony with one another, few persons desire to interfere with the traditional separation between church and state and give rise to sectarian strife. Above all, no responsible faculty member wants to admit dictation from without concerning the appointment of colleagues and the introduction of new courses and degree requirements. The problems concerned admit of no easy solution. A good beginning would perhaps be made if the universities themselves took the initiative and introduced informational undergraduate courses of high quality concerning the major faiths — a course for each religion and not a catch-all course in comparative religion — and also top-level graduate courses on the theology of those faiths. These courses, both undergraduate and graduate, should be taught by outstanding representatives of the respective faiths who would be selected by the universities and, subject to appropriate ecclesiastical concurrence, incorporated into their teaching staffs. Such teachers should not be confused with the all-important chaplains, who are charged with ministering to the spiritual and moral needs of students. The courses on religion that are open to undergraduates could be included within a group of courses one or more of which must be taken in fulfillment of the requirements for the bachelor's degree. By thus including religion under "general education" or other appropriate heading, the colleges would permit the courses to be counted toward a degree by those who elected to take them, and no student would be forced to take them.

The Greater Boston area continues to give evidence of its religious vitality. The Harvard Divinity School recently created the Charles Chauncey Stillman Guest Professorship of Roman Catholic Theological Studies, made possible by the generosity of Chauncey Devereux Stillman of the Harvard College Class of 1929 in honor of his father, who graduated from Harvard in 1898, and a Professorship of World Religions, founded by means of an anonymous gift. The Massachusetts Institute of Technology has constructed a simple but imposing chapel for all faiths; Catholic, Protestant, Jewish, Greek Orthodox, and Vedanta services are regularly held. Brandeis University has erected three magnificent chapels appropriately known merely as The Three Chapels. Similar in design and grouped around a heart-shaped lake in such a way that no one chapel dominates the other two, they are the Berlin Chapel, for students of the Jewish faith, the John Marshall Harlan Chapel for those of the Protestant faith, and the Bethlehem Chapel for Catholic students.

Yet another problem, one that has recently confronted American educators for the first time, is the proper timing of military service within the over-all educational process. No clear solution can be found until there is agreement on what the nature of the military service should be. In the meantime the students themselves are trying to solve the problem. Some do their service between high school and college and others after college. Still others enter graduate school and postpone their service even longer, assuming that the specialized knowledge they acquire will place them in a different relationship vis-à-vis the military.

The whole question of military service points up the need for solution to an urgent problem that affects all levels of education in the United States. This problem, the last that can be discussed in this chapter, concerns the desirability of compressing the educational process into a shorter span of years. Prior to the advent of military service an American went to school for twelve or thirteen years before entering college; college added four more, by which time the student was twenty-one, and graduate work added one, two, three, four, or even more years. Now military service of two or more years' duration must be added to the total.

It is obvious that something has to be given up. As it cannot be any of the years of military service, unless weapons operated by push-buttons reduce manpower requirements, it must come from the years in school or college. How can an acceleration or compression of education be effected? Two traditional methods of acceleration have been tried over the years and have proved both undesirable from an educational and health point of view and, apparently, relatively unpopular with the students. One is attendance at college throughout the year by taking advantage of summer schools, a process that is doubly costly, for the student must pay out money to attend summer school and at the same time give up any possibility of earning money during the summer months. The other method is the overloading of one's program, when permitted by the college authorities, by taking an excessive number of courses and so attaining the degree in less than the normal number of years.

Recent thinking on this problem has

recognized that some secondary schools obviously do a far better job of teaching than others and that some students are brighter or work harder, or both, than others. Therefore the better institutions and students should be rewarded. Four ways are possible, and all four are being tried on a limited scale. A first way is to admit a highly qualified secondary-school student direct from the end of the junior year in school to the freshman year of college (so-called Admission without Diploma). A second way is to admit a well qualified graduating senior to one or more advanced college courses in his freshman year (so-called Advanced Placement). Another way is to admit a well qualified gradu-ating senior direct to the sophomore year of college (so-called Sophomore Standing). Yet another way is to allow an outstanding student already in college who gives evidence that he was well prepared by his school to omit a college year. The University of Chicago long ago introduced programs whereby students might speed up their education. That pioneering spirit has now spread, and the present-day experiments may well establish a new pattern for the future. At Harvard, Admission without Diploma, Advanced Placement, and Sophomore Standing have been formalized into what is known as the Program of Advanced Standing and are rapidly winning acceptance.

V

Personnel Problems in American Higher Education

TEACHING AT the level of higher edu-cation is a distinct profession in the American scheme of things. Such teach-ing, which is closely related to research, is completely separated from elemen-tary- and secondary-school teaching. The training required for a career in the elementary and secondary schools is quite different from the preparation demanded for college and university teaching. In contrast to what happens in, for example, the French educational system, an American high-school teach-er rarely leaves secondary-school teach-ing to join a college faculty. This may or may not be a defect in the system. I am inclined to believe that it is not. American secondary-school teachers enter their profession with their eyes open and with the full intention of dedicating their lives to the teaching of adolescents; they are not preoccupied with time-consuming activities designed to get them out of that profession. In Chapter VII details are given concern-ing the professional training of ele-mentary- and secondary-school teach-ers.

The profession of teaching at the higher levels is subdivided according to the schools and faculties. This chap-ter is not concerned with purely pro-fessional teaching, of law, medicine, engineering, and the like, but rather with the teaching done in the liberal-arts colleges and, in the case of uni-versities, in the closely associated gradu-ate schools of arts and sciences.

From the point of view of personnel, the organization of the American sys-tem of higher education presents two major problems.

In the first place, an individual who wishes to teach within this system must decide between teaching in an independent liberal-arts college and teaching as a member of a university faculty of arts and sciences. If he chooses the latter, he will, of course, normally have an opportunity to teach both undergraduates and graduate students simultaneously. Just as the student must choose between an independent liberal-arts college and a university college, so a faculty member must also choose. There are professors who prefer to teach exclusively at the college level. They are interested in young men, or young women, from eighteen to twenty-one years of age and in general educational problems; they are less fascinated by the minutiae of a research career. For such persons, college teaching is preferable. Unfortunately, it does not pay as well as university teaching, although there may be additional compensations, such as low-cost housing provided by the college. Moreover, it is rather difficult to move from an independent college to a university faculty, for the many demands made upon faculty members prevent their doing the kind of publication and other scholarly activity that would attract a university's attention and lead to a call to a university post. Thus there is a dilemma for the young teacher, who does not know whether to choose the college or the university. As a matter of fact, the choice is not completely free. Those persons who give greatest promise of a scholarly research career are generally invited by universities; the others, and among them some very able teachers, are invited by the colleges.

In the second place, in a university faculty the energy of the professor is divided between college teaching, in which he must face a host of problems peculiar to this level of instruction, and graduate teaching, which is presumably close to his private research. The professor is obviously interested in his research and quite naturally often feels more drawn to that than to the college portion of his teaching duties. He must learn to combine the two types of activity, and to accept both of them as equal obligations. The advantages of the combination of the two types have already been discussed in Chapter II.

A person who wishes to enter the academic profession at the college or university level normally seeks admission to a graduate school of arts and sciences immediately upon receiving the baccalaureate. At times he waits a year, or even longer. In my opinion, however, it is preferable not to lose any time between the college and the graduate programs.

Graduate programs aim to prepare college and university teachers and also researchers. It must be remembered that the graduate school not only prepares teachers but also the specialists who go into industrial and governmental research. It also prepares some individuals for a literary or other creative career. Because of the variety in the interests of graduate students, the common core is research and not pedagogy. From the point of view of college teaching, this may well represent a defect, one that is discussed elsewhere.

The graduate school confers the traditional degree of Doctor of Philosophy (Ph.D.), which is usually required for college and university teaching. The program lasts for from four to six or more years. The length of time is wholly secondary; everything depends upon the graduate student's prior preparation and the nature of his subject. Normally he spends about two years taking courses, which are for the most part highly specialized courses or seminars. He then takes a general examination designed to test his knowledge of his field so that he can demonstrate his fitness to teach it at the college level; the examination is either all written or a combination of oral and written. He then writes a thesis or dissertation, in which he makes a small research contribution but in which he is primarily expected to demonstrate his fitness to do independent research and to prepare courses based on first-hand knowledge. After defending his thesis in a final oral examination, he receives the doctorate.

It is obviously highly desirable that practice teaching be an integral part of the graduate training of future teachers. Consequently, as many graduate students as university resources permit teach for one or more years under the direction of a regular faculty member. They normally teach on a part-time basis, for three or six or nine hours a week, the balance of their time being devoted to formal study. These apprentice teachers are called Teaching Fellows or Teaching Assistants. They are paid at a rate that varies from about $3,000 to $4,400 a year, but as they rarely teach full time, they are paid only for the fraction of time during which they actually teach, quarter-time, third-time, half-time, and so forth. Graduate students who are not awarded teaching fellowships or assistantships by the graduate school in which they are studying often have an opportunity of doing teaching in a neighboring institution, thus acquiring valuable teaching experience. Still other graduate students have had teaching experience prior to embarking on their Ph.D. program.

One graduate school has announced a double scale for its Teaching Fellows beginning in 1960–1961: a full-time rate of $4,200 for those who have not completed their basic course work (that is, completed the so-called "residence requirement"), $5,400 for those who have done so.

For many people outside the United States who are accustomed to evaluate a doctorate exclusively in terms of the thesis or theses presented for it, the American Ph.D. is a strange degree. Actually, it represents far more than a thesis. It is a sign of rigorous training in subject-matter, research techniques, and writing, to a lesser degree in teaching. In other words, the American Ph.D. degree should be viewed in terms of the holder, the man or woman, and not exclusively in terms of a thesis.

Even though graduate-school programs are frequently criticized for overemphasizing research and neglecting teacher preparation, the research training itself does not seem to be adequate, and there is a growing tendency for the able young Ph.D.'s to seek postdoctoral research fellowships from one of the philanthropic foundations in order to be able to bring to a conclusion a major research project before settling down in a regular academic position. The foundations, incidentally, and also other fellowship-awarding agencies, seem to favor such postdoctoral full-time research, especially if it bridges traditional academic disciplines.

For the young man or woman who has attained the doctorate, the normal university hierarchy is the following: Instructor, Assistant Professor, Associate Professor, and Professor, the latter often known colloquially as a "full" Professor.

The terms of appointments and salaries of Instructors and Assistant

Cornell University, Ithaca, New York: Willard Straight Hall (student union)

Brandeis University, Waltham, Massachusetts: The Three Chapels.

Bryn Mawr College, Bryn Mawr, Pennsylvania: Campus scene.

The Catholic University of America, Washington, District of Columbia: Mullen Memorial Library (center), Shahan Hall, School of Social Service (left), Keane Physics Research Center (right).

Assumption College, Worcester, Massachusetts: Campus, with Maison
Francaise in left foreground.

Yale University, New Haven, Connecticut: Sterling Memorial Library.

Harvard University, Cambridge, Massachusetts: Harkness Commons of Graduate Student Center, with Law School in background.

Williams College, Williamstown, Massachusetts: Griffin Hall, for classes, lectures, and faculty meetings.

California Institute of Technology, Pasadena, California: Synchrotron.

University of Michigan, Ann Arbor, Michigan: Medical Center.

Stanford University, Stanford, California: The Hoover Institution on War, Revolution, and Peace.

Professors vary considerably in different colleges and universities. Perhaps the only generalization that can safely be made is that the Instructors are appointed for one year at a time, whereas the Assistant Professors receive appointments of more than one year, for three years, for instance, or for five. The Instructor's salary varies from perhaps as little as $3,500 to $6,500 and that of the Assistant Professor from $4,000 to $8,500 or more.

At many institutions promotion to an Associate Professorship carries with it life tenure, and of course the full Professor normally has tenure. In an institution in which the Associate as well as the full Professor is appointed for life, the difference between these two ranks is primarily one of prestige and of salary. The duties are similar. Indeed, in general the American academic hierarchy is one of salaries and length of time in several ranks and not a hierarchy of responsibilities. Thus a twenty-five-year-old Instructor could easily have the full responsibility of a graduate course of his own. American teachers, regardless of rank, do not have exclusive rights to a carefully delimited field, to a "chair" in the sense in which the term is used in some European and Latin-American countries.

The salaries of the permanent staff vary greatly in the United States. In colleges and small universities, they range from $5,000 or even less to $8,000 or $9,000. In larger universities they may go from $7,000 to $25,000 per year. In general the small private colleges pay the lowest salaries and the great private universities the highest. In addition to the purely financial compensation, there is a practice in American higher education which makes teaching in many colleges and universi-

ties very attractive. It is the system of sabbatical leave. Every seven years the Professor may have leave for the full academic year at half-pay or for one-half of the year at full pay. At Harvard University, the Assistant Professor, who has a five-year appointment, enjoys one term of leave during his five years.

In addition to cash salaries, normally paid for nine months of teaching, faculty members often receive "fringe benefits," paid-up pensions, low-rate life insurance, low-cost family medical plans, scholarships for children, low-cost housing, and free use of recreational and cultural facilities.

When it is remembered that the salary scales of the vast majority of American institutions of higher learning are at the low end of the ranges given above, it becomes obvious that a major problem facing American education is that of attracting the highest type of personnel to the academic profession, to higher education, and also to elementary and secondary education. The college student gives considerable thought to his future; if he does not, his parents do. What will he do after graduating? Will he go directly into business? Will he enter a professional school and study medicine or law? These are weighty matters for the college senior, who is helped by his college placement bureau or vocational guidance center. An important factor in his decision is salary, or potential salary. The young man knows, or at least believes, that teaching does not pay as well as the other professions, not nearly as well as business. There are compensations, it is true, or so he thinks: freedom, an agreeable life, the satisfaction of personal interests. Still, there is that question of salary.

A great mistake made by several American universities since World War

II, namely, of raising the salaries of Instructors and Assistant Professors out of all proportion to the amount by which the salaries of permanent Professors were raised, has added to the difficulties of recruiting teaching personnel. Able young men, while of course interested in the immediate salary, also have an eye to the future and note that the possibility of substantial raises is rather slight in most colleges and universities.

In order to attract qualified men to the teaching profession, Princeton University has rendered American education a signal service. In 1945 it established a series of fellowships, the Woodrow Wilson National Fellowships, which have as their goal to contribute to a young man's decision to enter the academic profession. Princeton recognized that the other professions have sufficient attractions, real or imagined, especially financial attractions. The new fellowships are supposed to compensate for the lack of financial rewards in the academic profession in the sense that they finance the first year of the professional training of the future teacher. They are offered to individuals who are carefully selected, after personal interview, from among those nominated by responsible faculty members as being the type of student who should be recruited into the profession. The fellowship allows the student to give the profession a try for a year. The program, now administered by the Woodrow Wilson National Fellowship Foundation, awards one thousand fellowships per year, mostly in the non-science fields. It is thus the largest non-governmental awarder of fellowships.

In many universities, the salary for each rank has been the same regardless of the teacher's field. The professor of classical archaeology has received the same remuneration as the professor of atomic physics. In view of the greatly increased demand in recent years on the part of both government and industry for scientists, it is almost inevitable that institutions of higher education enter the competition for the scientists. By so doing, they create a salary differential and, in turn, a host of new problems.

American teachers normally work full time for the university or college that employs them, although in the professional schools practitioners of the profession concerned often do some teaching. Many full-time professors do earn extra money, from consultant's fees paid by government, foundations, or industry, from book royalties, especially textbook royalties, from lecture fees, from teaching in summer school or in university extension, and the like. The amount of money that professors earn in addition to their basic salary varies considerably. Consultants receive from $50 to $1,000 a day, $100 to $300 being typical for scientists and engineers. The nature of their subject prevents some professors from being invited as consultants. They are not in a position to write books that sell many copies. Yet, even though they are in exotic subjects, they can popularize them in paid public lectures or by well-written books.

The distribution of posts among the several disciplines is often a problem in an American university faculty, especially in times when student interests shift, or concentrate on four or five fields. In a few universities each department has a fixed number of permanent posts and a fixed number of assistant professorships. Thus, continuity in the teaching of and research in all branches of knowledge is assured, in spite of variation in student interest. From the point of view of personnel the system is excellent in that the younger men are enabled to plan their futures with some knowledge of whether vacancies lie ahead of them in their own university.

In a system that is as vast and complex as higher education in the United States the problem of selecting teachers for initial appointment and for promotion is about the most basic. In the universities, the single most important criterion appears to be publication, proof of solid scholarship. There is a standing joke which declares that a book weighing two pounds is worth an assistant professorship and one weighing five pounds a permanent appointment. In American universities it is very difficult to take into consideration factors such as teaching ability, personality, breadth of knowledge. There is reluctance to visit a younger teacher's classes and "spy on" his teaching performance. There is also a certain hesitation in accepting student opinion, especially as obtained through polling techniques. As a result, recourse is had to published writings, and also to the personal opinions of friends in other institutions who know the candidate in question.

As for the mechanics of selection, the members of the department that needs a new teacher are already acquainted with the men in the field, largely through the latters' writings or their appearance at national meetings. They make a list of possible candidates, study their articles and books, and make a recommendation to the dean; they often have to defend their recommendation before the central university administration.

So far the system of appointment has been described from the point of view of the university — the university calls or invites a person to be a professor. The young Ph.D.'s just out of graduate school also exercise some initiative of their own and look for positions, often with the assistance of the school's placement or appointment office. Moreover, and most important of all, the head or chairman of the department in which the job seeker did his graduate work makes every effort to help him secure a suitable position. Graduate students visit other universities and attend national congresses of specialists, reading papers to attract attention. Because of this materialistic aspect of the national meetings, the latter are humorously referred to as "slave markets." Professor So-and-so of X University takes his best student to the market in order to auction him off to the university that bids highest in terms of salary, possibility of promotion, and opportunity of teaching the young man's special field.

To educators in countries that have rigid public examinations for doctoral candidates and an equally rigid publicly supervised system of selection of professors, the American system must appear singularly haphazard and personal. Its nature is all the more surprising as every effort is made to ensure equal opportunity for the admission of students to colleges and universities. It is undoubtedly true that American universities do have much to learn from other countries concerning personnel selection and promotion.

As was pointed out in Chapter II, relations between faculty and administration in American institutions of higher learning are in general excellent. There is little of the labor-management friction that is found in industry. Teachers' unions exist but their role in many institutions is rather limited, primarily because the problems that interest them also interest the university administrations and there consequently is little conflict. The American Association of University Professors (A.A.U.P.), an organization that is just what its name implies, is an association of great prestige in the United States and is especially effective in being on the alert against encroachments on life tenure and academic freedom.

There is a final personnel problem: retirement. The normal retirement age is sixty-five or sixty-six, although on occasion exceptional faculty members who are able to continue their duties are invited to remain on the active list a few more years. The retired or emeritus professor receives a pension for the rest of his life. The amount of the pension is dependent upon the amount of money put into the pension plan, either by the individual, his institution, or both, during the teacher's career. A perhaps not uncommon goal is to have the amount of the annual pension equal to one-half of the professor's average annual salary during his last ten years of active service. A typical pension plan functions as follows: the university withholds 5 per cent of the teacher's salary for his

pension and itself puts in an equivalent amount, or else puts in an amount equal to 7.5 per cent or even 10 per cent of the salary figure. Some universities have their own pension plans. For faculty members in other institutions there is a national insurance plan set up exclusively for teachers, the Teachers Insurance and Annuity Association (T.I.A.A.). Professors in state or municipal universities are usually considered to be government employees and consequently come under state or city pension plans. Moreover, the federal Social Security laws make college and university staffs eligible for social security over and above other pension provisions.

A new practice has been introduced in the United States in recent years: when a distinguished professor with a large salary retires from his university, he may be invited to teach for a few years on a reduced schedule by another, sometimes smaller, college or university that cannot afford to pay large salaries and therefore does not have, or would not otherwise have, the most distinguished faculty possible.

VI

The Financing of Higher Education in the United States

IT IS a commonplace to say that education costs money. Almost everyone recognizes that education is most important for the individual, for society, and for national defense. Unfortunately, the dreams of the educational thinkers are not realized because society and governments do not contribute sufficient money. In the United States

the financial problem is enormous because of the vastness of the educational system and because new ideas are often put into practice before sufficient funds are available to support them.

American colleges and universities are either public or private, that is, supported by public funds or supported privately, by a church group or other groups acting as private citizens although under a state charter.

A public institution is owned and operated by a government, either a state or a municipal government. The government appropriates large sums of money for the institution's expenses. Yet these sums are normally not sufficient to cover all expenses, and so the institution is partially dependent on student fees and on gifts. In order to obtain needed revenue, most state universities charge only a nominal tuition to students from the same state but, as has been noted, charge a much higher fee for out-of-state students. With respect to finances, such universities are quite literally state universities and not national institutions. The matter of states rights and the autonomy of the states in educational questions is discussed in Chapter IX.

A private institution receives no direct financial aid from any government, municipal, state, or federal. The money used to pay the operating expenses has a threefold origin: tuition fees paid by students; money given in the form of gifts for immediate use; and the income from invested capital in the possession of the institution and often originally received by the institution in the form of gifts to be invested, with only the income to be spent.

In general terms, the older private universities have relatively large "endowment," that is, income-producing capital. They charge high tuition fees, $800, $900, $1,000, even $1,200 or $1,300 a year just for instruction; this sum does not include food, room, medical fee, books, traveling expenses, or sundry personal expenses. Moreover, because the families of students in private universities often have more money than those of the students in public universities, the students, especially after graduation, contribute large sums in the form of gifts. There is thus a threefold compensation for the lack of public support. Yet troubles lie ahead. Income taxes and inheritance taxes are high and consequently make it difficult to accumulate fortunes. The federal income-tax laws are such, however, that gifts given to educational institutions may be deducted from an individual's income for tax-paying purposes, up to a total of 30 per cent of the income. Even so, private universities are already facing grave financial problems.

The private colleges and universities have been reluctant to raise their tuition any more, for they feel that if they do so the students will go to the public institutions, where tuition is much less, ranging from a few dollars to perhaps $400 or $500. In the past two or three years, however, they have in fact raised the tuition fee considerably and with the avowed purpose of raising faculty salaries. One argument in justification of this increase stresses the economic benefits of higher education to the individual. The student must invest in himself, it is argued, and be willing to borrow large sums, if necessary. A counter-argument states that the economic and social benefits flow primarily to all of society, so a variety of means should finance higher education.

A private university that has little endowment and few gifts unfortunately must either have a high tuition fee or keep its expenses down. The latter course can mean a lowering of the quality of instruction. The professors receive less money; the libraries buy fewer books; the laboratories become antiquated; the students receive little scholarship aid.

Private universities not only do not receive money from governments but, in the past at least, they have tended not to want to accept public funds. The first reason is that private universities, with an assured income year after year from endowments, gifts, and tuition charges, are able to make long-range plans and do not favor short-term budgets, such as, for instance, the two-year budgets under which many public universities operate. The second and vastly more important reason private universities have not wanted government money is that they fear an inevitable control which would quite naturally, and perhaps necessarily, accompany the taxpayers' money. They prize their academic freedom so much that they do not like the idea of restrictions and conditions from government.

Although it is true that a private educational institution receives no direct financial aid from government, it receives, and is extremely grateful for, considerable indirect aid. Mention has already been made of one feature of the income-tax laws that aids education. Another feature of these laws exempts educational institutions from paying income tax on the income they receive from their endowments and other sources. Moreover, the property belonging to educational institutions and used for educational purposes is exempt from local real-estate taxes.

There are other types of indirect financial aid. Thus, when the federal government aids a group of students on a nationwide basis, for instance, the war veterans mentioned in Chapter I, or future naval officers, or future scientists (who are aided on a vast national scale by a program administered by the National Science Foundation), all colleges and universities, public and private, benefit. The money is paid to or on behalf of the individual and not to the institution as such. The individual may select his institution and, usually, his program. Private institutions recognize more and more that they need government aid and naturally prefer assistance of this indirect type because the danger of government control is reduced to a minimum.

Another indirect, and slight, contribution recently made to education by society via the federal government concerns the income tax. A child, regardless of age, who for at least five months during a calendar year is a full-time student at an educational institution qualifies as a dependent, regardless of his own earnings, provided the parent-taxpayer furnishes more than half his support. The parent may therefore deduct $600 from his income for each such student and consequently pay less tax. If the child earns $600 or more he must still, of course, file his own income tax return. A fellowship or scholarship received by the student from an educational institution or other agency is not, however, counted as income and is therefore not taxable.

American colleges and universities have one minor difficulty with gifts, gifts given generously by private citizens or by industry either to increase capital endowment or for immediate use. The philanthropists who give so generously of their money (the gifts range from two dollars to fifteen million dollars) frequently specify the use to which their money will be put. Such a stipulation is normally perfectly satisfactory, as the institution may be endeavoring to raise money for just that purpose and the donation may be made in response to the campaign. At times, however, restricted gifts can be embarrassing and may, in the long run, be quite costly to an institution. Thus, money may be given to endow a chair in a new subject. The income is just sufficient to pay the salary of the new professor. Yet, in order for him to teach the new subject effectively, the library will have to buy books in that field, and assistant will have to be provided, and scholarship funds will have to be made available for new students of the subject. All of these costs will have to be borne by the institution out of its other funds. Similarly, money may be given for a new building, with no provision for its upkeep. Consequently the institutions of higher learning are giving more and more publicity to their specific needs and are emphasizing the desirability of unrestricted gifts.

Within a university, the alumni of the liberal-arts college respond the most generously, largely, perhaps, because of the sentimental attachment, already referred to in Chapter III, that most American alumni retain for their undergraduate college. It often happens that an American will go to college in one university and to graduate school in another; he will normally make what financial contributions he can to the former and not to the latter, although the latter will have given him his professional training, the direct means whereby he will earn the money to give! From a purely selfish point of view universities might encourage their college alumni to go to graduate school in the same university. They do not, however, for it is generally considered to be broadening to attend more than one institution.

The role of the foundations — Rockefeller, Carnegie, Guggenheim, and Ford — in supporting American higher education is enormous. Their generosity extends to a large number of areas. The foundations give grants directly to individual professors to support research. They also give money to universities for distribution by the university authorities for research purposes. They provide traveling fellowships for students and faculty members. They make grants to institutions to aid in developing a new subject or a new approach to older subjects. In the case of such grants, the money given is usually only enough to initiate the project; once it is under way, after one year or perhaps five years, the foundation expects the institution itself to finance its continuation. Consequently, a financially well-administered university is careful to accept foundation aid only for those continuing projects that it feels it will be able to finance in the future.

The generosity of foundations toward education is exemplified by the Ford Foundation. The vast majority of its expenditures have been invested in educational improvement, directly or indirectly, including the improvement of teaching. The Ford Foundation has considered the most urgent need in education to be the increase in the supply and the improvement in the utilization of superior teachers. Its program in education has stressed means of meeting this need.

In spite of the generosity of foundations and regardless of the continuing loyal support of individual donors, large and small, higher education in the United States would have been in dire financial straits and would perhaps have been forced to be receptive to direct government support if a new source of financial aid had not suddenly appeared. This new source is business and industry, that is, the private corporations. Business and industry now recognize that they, too, have a huge stake in higher education, in the training of potential employees, executives, and researchers, and in the basic or fundamental research of a type that can best be done by universities. They therefore are giving large sums to colleges and universities, and it is hoped that they will give a considerably higher proportion of their earnings in the future.

The sudden increase in "corporate giving," as it is called, is principally due to a court decision of a few years ago. This decision held that the giving, within reasonable limits, of unrestricted funds out of a corporation's profits to an educational institution is legal, for such expenditures are in reality for the long-range benefit of the corporation.

Lest the contributions made by corporations form a haphazard and even unjust pattern, some persons believe an effort should be made to band some institutions together and have the corporations give to the resulting association, which would then, in turn, make a distribution to its members. A beginning has been made in this direction, and there is already in existence, for example, a New England Colleges Fund, Inc., which is affiliated with an American College Fund.

These contributions made by business and industry to higher education are quite independent of money made available to higher education by research contracts between industrial and business corporations and universities. These contracts, and similar contracts between the federal government and universities, have become an important element in the research as well as financial life of many institutions. Each contract is scrutinized with care by responsible university officials, however, for there is an ever-present temptation to accept contracts which might direct university researchers' efforts away from basic research and toward applied research, which many educators believe should be held to a minimum in universities.

If American educators object to governmental control of education and consequently tend not to desire financial aid from government, why, it may be asked, do they solicit and accept support from private industry, which may attempt to exert pressures and expect favorable consideration in return for its favors? Educators are well aware of the dangers here and endeavor to set up every safeguard before accepting funds. Moreover, the danger of industrial control is probably much smaller than that from government, for industry is divided. No single corporation rivals the federal government in financial strength.

The finances of a university are usually centralized in the office of the treasurer, a most important official who is responsible for investing his institution's capital funds. He may also be responsible for the over-all budget, or this duty may be performed by another official, the president himself, or possibly an administrative vice-president. In any event the budget must ultimately be approved by the president and the trustees. It is prepared at lower levels and reaches the president in summary form. Inasmuch as, in some American universities, each faculty is more or less autonomous, it prepares its own budget for the president's approval. Within the faculty, each department prepares its budget, which includes teachers' salaries, employees' salaries, necessary supplies and equipment, printing, stationery, postage, telephone, and so forth. The dean of the faculty assembles the department budgets. It is he who balances them because it is usually he, and not the department chairmen, who knows how much endowment and tuition income is being credited to his faculty. Each balanced faculty budget then goes higher up and is coordinated with central administrative budgets for final approval.

The financing of American colleges and universities is both complicated and interesting. There is the greatest good will in the administration of the finances, especially in private universities. University treasurers, some of whom devote considerable time and energy to this work without salary, deserve the highest praise.

American philanthropists of both past and present likewise deserve the highest praise. These generous individuals have a great sense of social responsibility and are desirous of bettering the lot of the average citizen. They give money to establish professorships; to build laboratories, libraries, museums, chapels and religious centers, gymnasiums, dormitories, and classroom buildings; to buy books; to establish scholarships and fellowships and loan and beneficiary aid funds, beneficiary aid being money given to students in small amounts to cover sudden emergencies; to create emergency funds for the personal use of the faculty; and so on. They well deserve the honorary degrees they often receive at commencement exercises.

The perusal of the list of scholarships and fellowships offered by almost any sizeable American college or university is a moving experience because the list shows the sublime generosity of education's benefactors.

An example: Senator Leverett Saltonstall, of an old New England family long devoted to Harvard, lost a son during World War II; he was killed in action on the island of Guam. The boy's family gave $89,000 to Harvard to establish a memorial scholarship for a student from the general region where his son fought. This scholarship is available to assist a worthy student from the Hawaiian Islands and those islands west of Hawaii, including New Zealand, the Fiji Islands, and Australia, in obtaining an education in any department of the University. The purpose of this memorial is to further the education, the health, and the welfare of the peoples inhabiting these regions of the far Pacific.

Another example: A young man graduated from Harvard College and entered the United States Marine Corps. He was killed in the attack on the Marianas in 1944. An anonymous donor gave Harvard $25,000 "to establish a scholarship in memory of the late Captain David A. Kelleher, Jr., U.S. Marine Corps, Harvard A.B. (*cum laude*) 1941."

A last example is a quotation from the deed of gift of a proud and grateful father: "My sons, Capt. Richard Witkin, Harvard College, 1939, and First Lieutenant William Isaac Witkin, University of North Carolina, 1943, were both first pilots of B-24 Liberators in the Fifteenth Air Force. Each successfully completed fifty missions, received the Air Medal with numerous clusters and the Distinguished Flying Cross. In gratitude for and in commemoration of their safe return from combat I would like to create a modest scholarship at their respective colleges. . . . I would like to have the income therein made available to any undergraduate student in the College in any manner the authorities direct."

VII

Professional Training in American Colleges

and Universities

HIGHER EDUCATION in the United States has two complementary responsibilities: the general education of citizens and the professional training of persons with the necessary qualifications. In broad outline, general education, normally combined with pre-professional preparation, is the function of the undergraduate colleges of liberal arts, and professional education is the function of the graduate schools. There are, however, as was pointed out at the beginning of Chapter II, some professional colleges at the undergraduate level. Indeed, from the point of view of significance to contemporary American life, these undergraduate professional colleges, and also a vast number of technological and vocational colleges, schools, and institutes that require a high-school diploma for admission, are most important. The role of the state agricultural colleges, for example, is vital to the American economy. As an instance of how the ordinary citizen may be made aware of them, mention could be made of the agricultural experiment stations that these colleges maintain in many parts of the country, stations whose highly trained staffs are most helpful in furnishing advice without charge to homeowners who are troubled with bugs and beetles in their flower and vegetable gardens.

This chapter will discuss in very brief form the training given for several of the professions; space does not permit inclusion of all of them. As will be noted, there is a common thread running through most American professional programs, namely, the necessity for more of what is now called "general education." When the professional training is at the undergraduate level, as in engineering, general education is an integral part of the program. When it is at the graduate level, a general undergraduate preparation is normally required for admission, and not a technical or overspecialized college program.

Teaching. Chapter V included a discussion of the training of American college and university teachers. The present statements cover only the preparation of elementary- and secondary-school teachers.

Elementary-school teachers are generally prepared by the teachers colleges, formerly known as "normal schools," although there is a trend toward elementary-teacher education in state universities and private liberal-arts colleges as well. The teachers colleges may be municipal but are usually state. Their program lasts four years and terminates with a bachelor's degree.

Elementary education has been a great problem in the United States. The teachers were not well paid. They had little prestige. In recent years, however, there has been an important change in elementary teaching. The average salary is more than double what it used to be, and the prestige of the teachers has risen. Moreover, the average salary of elementary-school teachers more nearly approaches that of the secondary-school teachers than formerly. The explanation is partly sociological and of great interest as showing a possible influence of Freudian studies. It is being increasingly recognized that the influences to which a child is subjected in his formative years are very lasting. Consequently, an influential segment of the public is demanding that the teaching in the early elementary grades be as good as possible and is willing to pay the salaries needed to attract the best-qualified persons as teachers. There is, moreover, increasing recognition of the need for a rich and broad liberal-arts background for the elementary-school teachers since the very nature of their teaching embraces the entire range of subject matter. As a result of this recognition, the teachers colleges as such are disappearing and being supplanted by liberal-arts colleges.

Secondary-school teachers are generally prepared by the colleges of liberal arts. They follow the regular program leading to the Bachelor of Arts or Bachelor of Science degree. They have a "major" or field of concentration just like other students, and, if they are fortunate, they will teach this same subject after they become teachers. There is one difference between the bachelor's program for future secondary-school teachers and that for the others. In the former, a certain number of courses in "education" or pedagogy are required, such as history of education, philosophy of education, educational measurements, educational psychology, and practice teaching, the last of which the students obtain in a secondary school close to the college and affiliated with it for this purpose. These courses in education are required by the states in the United States as part of the preparation for teaching in the public secondary schools; they are beginning to be required by the private preparatory schools.

Some college students who intend to enter secondary-school teaching prefer to follow the normal baccalaureate program, omitting the education courses, and then enter a graduate school of education and take the complete pedagogic training in one year, that is, the fifth university year, or else in a year and a summer. These individuals thus receive the bachelor's degree and also a master's degree. As salary increases in many municipal and state educational systems depend in large measure on advanced courses taken by the teacher, the master's degree is a coveted possession. Teachers who receive teaching posts without this degree often take summer-school courses in order to earn it.

Courses in education are not required as part of the preparation of college and university teachers, although the present dissatisfaction with this preparation alluded to in Chapter I may well lead to the requiring of some pedagogic training over and above the practice teaching that some graduate students now receive.

Because of a lack of properly qualified teachers in American schools, many colleges and universities as well as other agencies are publicizing among undergraduate students the career opportunities in education. They are stressing not only the nobility and general attractiveness of teaching but also the numerous and lucrative administrative posts open to capable persons with teaching experience.

Ministry. Members of the clergy are normally trained in seminaries, or theological or divinity schools. Many of these are graduate schools; the programs in some, however, include undergraduate studies. Some of them are independent; others form a part of universities.

Catholic priests are trained in diocesan seminaries, in seminaries belonging to religious orders, or in the school of theology of a Catholic university, such as the Catholic University of America in Washington, D.C. Protestant ministers receive their training in independent or university theological schools which may or may not be denominational. Rabbis are trained in Jewish theological seminaries.

Engineering. American engineers are normally trained in an engineering college within a university or in an independent engineering school or institute of technology. The ordinary program follows secondary school, is of four years' duration, and terminates with the bachelor's degree. Some engineering schools have advanced programs for engineers who wish additional training or who wish preparation for teaching or research. Students who complete such advanced training are awarded the master's or the doctor's degree.

The general education of American engineers is a constant preoccupation of engineering-school faculties. Thus some engineering schools are giving a much larger place in the curriculum to such subjects as English, history, and social science than formerly, recognizing that engineers should receive instruction in the type of society in which we live and in the impact on that society of engineering and general scientific development. Moreover, a number of the well-known engineering institutions have worked out a plan whereby certain liberal-arts colleges are affiliated with them; selected students of these latter colleges take part

of their training in the home institution and then enter the engineering institution with advanced standing, receiving degrees in both liberal arts and engineering.

Medicine. In the United States medicine is normally taught at the graduate level in a graduate school of medicine, which usually requires the bachelor's degree for admission. The formal medicine program lasts four years, and the degree received is that of Doctor of Medicine (M.D.). After leaving medical school, the young doctor must spend one or more years interning in a hospital, with the result that the over-all medical preparation lasts many years. In order to shorten this time, some universities allow their students to combine the fourth year of the liberal-arts college with the first year of medicine and award both the bachelor's degree and the M.D. for seven years of training.

Formerly the college program followed by students intending to go into medicine was rather narrow. It was called a premedical program, with a strong specialization in science, especially in the biological sciences. At present some medical schools have quite a different philosophy concerning premedical education. They believe that the college education should be general. They realize now that physicians are going to be citizens in a community and not just practitioners of medicine. They are aware that an important part of medicine is the physician's ability to converse with his patients, to understand the psychological, sociological, and human aspects of the patients' case histories. Therefore, these medical schools do the scientific teaching: they want their students to have had a broad general education. For admission they merely require one year of physics, two years of chemistry, and one year of biology.

The education of physicians in the United States is an enormous problem, just as it is in other countries. The medical profession wishes to maintain high medical standards. To prepare physicians adequately is very expensive. Because of the emphasis on quality, there are few medical schools, and the number of students is relatively small. There are only 85 approved medical schools, with some 30,000 students. In 1905 there were 160 schools with 26,000 students. The reduction does not signify a diminution of interest in medicine. On the contrary, it represents an effort to eliminate the inferior schools. As a result, in a country of 170,000,000 inhabitants 7,500 doctors of medicine are trained each year.

The solution to the problem is not easy. Money with which to establish more medical schools is lacking. Money is also lacking for medical scholarships, which are very necessary because the tuition fee in medical schools is often high, $1,500 per year in some. Moreover, there exists within the American medical profession the feeling that the quality of American medicine might not be maintained if the number of schools and of students were greatly increased.

Law. The description of law programs in the United States is complicated by two factors. In the first place, law can be either federal law or state law, public law being in general federal and private law in general state law. The lawyer is admitted to the practice of his profession by the state in which he resides. The examinations for admission to practice, the so-called bar examinations, are given by the state. Therefore, a good law school must take account of state law in its curriculum and yet must also base a large part of its instruction on federal law. In the second place, there is a difference between the narrow preparation of the student for the state bar examinations and his broad and theoretical preparation for the practice of an old and venerable profession. The good law school emphasizes the broader aspects of law in general.

The law schools of greatest prestige in the United States are at the graduate level and normally require the bachelor's degree for admission. The curriculum is of three years' duration, and the graduate receives the degree of Bachelor of Laws (LL.B.).

The better law schools have the same philosophy as the better medical schools as far as college preparation is concerned. They want this preparation to be broad and general and not overspecialized in economics or other social sciences.

In recent years American law schools have greatly increased the scope of their activities. Far from being local schools concerned exclusively with regional problems, they are now giant international centers. Some offer courses in International Legal Studies in which lawyers from abroad are encouraged to enroll. They often award special advanced degrees for successful completion of these studies.

Architecture. Students desiring to enter the architectural profession may enroll in colleges of architecture at the undergraduate level within some universities and attain an architectural degree after four or, more normally, five years of training. They may also obtain their professional training at the graduate level after completion of an entire undergraduate liberal-arts program. The degree of Bachelor of Architecture (B.Arch.) is usually the first degree in architecture. Advanced degrees, for instance, that of Master in Architecture (M.Arch.), are offered by many institutions.

Business. "One of the oldest of the arts and youngest of the professions," to quote the Harvard commencement ceremony, is business administration. Preparation for business can be very diverse. As is well known, formal education is not a prerequisite for a successful career in business. Yet education is more and more necessary for those who wish to attain executive positions. For this reason, in the United States there are schools of commerce, or business, or business administration. The colleges of business or commerce are at the undergraduate level, require a secondary-school education for admission, and award the bachelor's degree. Like the engineering schools, and for similar reasons, they include liberal subjects in their programs, humanities and social science.

Because of its pioneering work in many fields, the Harvard Graduate School of Business Administration merits perhaps more than passing mention. As its name implies, it is at the graduate level. Its program covers two years, terminating with the degree of Master in Business Administration (M.B.A.). The baccalaureate is normally required but is not absolutely necessary for admission. Four-fifths of the students who enter the school have had no previous schooling in business. Of those who are admitted, the largest group have had a liberal-arts background, while under 30 per cent have had engineering training. The Harvard program is not technical in the limited sense. It aims to lay a broad foundation for the future businessman, to

teach him how to reason, to use sound judgment, to solve complicated problems, problems whose solution requires the application of a number of branches of knowledge, above all the application of a knowledge of "human relations." Consequently, the school developed the subject that is known as human relations, and also applied the case method to the teaching of business administration. A true-life situation is studied from all points of view, human, sociological, economic, political, even scientific. The nucleus of this instruction is the situation, the case, and not an academic discipline.

Military service. In the traditional list of professions in the United States the average American would include teaching, medicine, the ministry (that is, theology), engineering, and law. He would probably not include the profession of arms, yet military service (Army, Navy, Air Force, Marine Corps) is a profession like any other and should be mentioned here.

The officers of the regular services are normally prepared in two famous academies, the Military Academy, in West Point, New York, and the Naval Academy, in Annapolis, Maryland, and in the new Air Force Academy located near Colorado Springs in the state of Colorado. The programs at these academies are at the college level and the graduates receive the bachelor's degree. At times graduates of these institutions leave the regular service and have splendid careers in business or industry. Those who stay in the service for permanent careers normally attend a wide variety of schools and courses, both civilian and military, including some at an advanced graduate level.

For the training of reserve officers, the several branches of the service depend in large measure on the undergraduate colleges. Many of these colleges have what is known as a Reserve Officers Training Corps (R.O.T.C.); there are three different ones, for Army, Navy, and Air, the Navy R.O.T.C. being also the training unit for Marine Corps reserve officers. The students follow a normal academic program and in addition take the military courses. They devote one or more summers to military training, and when they receive their bachelor's degree they may also receive an officer's commission, as a Second Lieutenant or Ensign.

In addition to West Point, Annapolis, the Air Force Academy, and the colleges with R.O.T.C. units, there is an additional source of officers — the military colleges, of which the Virginia Military Institute (V.M.I.) is an example. Many graduates of those colleges which offer a broad military program within their R.O.T.C. enter the regular military establishment with permanent officers' commissions.

Journalism. In the United States there are a number of excellent colleges of journalism, usually four-year undergraduate colleges awarding the bachelor's degree. Some of the more conservative universities, while very desirous of promoting good journalism in any way possible, have, however, been reluctant to establish such schools of journalism, preferring to believe that a broad general education in a good liberal-arts college is perhaps a better preparation for a career in journalism.

Professional licensing is a matter that rests with the states. Lawyers, engineers, physicians, and dentists must usually pass state examinations in order to be allowed to practice their respective professions. The examinations are passed only once, and thereafter the professional man is allowed to practice in his state as long as he acts within the ethics of his profession. If he moves to another state, he may or may not have to take a new examination, depending on the reciprocal agreements in effect between his old state and the new one.

Because licensing is a state activity, the degrees awarded by American colleges and universities carry in themselves no civil rights. They are thus legally no more than diplomas awarded by the educational institutions.

Although membership in professional associations such as the American Medical Association, the American Dental Association, and the American Bar Association, is not required as a prerequisite for licensing in the professions just mentioned, it may be required by some insurance companies before they will insure individuals who wish to protect themselves against suit for malpractice. Moreover, such membership is usually highly desirable in order that a professional man may keep abreast of developments in his field.

In engineering and in some of the other professions, the national professional associations play an important role in the accreditation of the programs of professional schools. Accreditation of liberal-arts colleges is discussed in Chapter IX.

In general, women in the United States do not enter the traditional professions, in spite of the concept of the American career girl that has been spread abroad, chiefly by the movies. Women may enter professional schools, however, and appear to be doing so in increasing numbers, although some of these schools have a certain hesitation about admitting them. Thus, if an already overcrowded medical school admits a woman student, making a considerable investment in her in money, time, and facilities, and blocking the admission of a man, and if she marries immediately after receiving her degree and practices medicine either not at all or only slightly, there is a distinct loss to the medical profession. The graduate schools of arts and sciences, on the other hand, admit women in large numbers, yet it is quite difficult, and in many institutions impossible, for a woman to be admitted to the faculty of a university, even a coeducational university, or of a liberal-arts college whose student body is all male.

VIII

The University Library in the United States

IT IS OBVIOUS that a good library is a prime necessity for a university. If an adequate public research library is in the neighborhood, as in Washington, Lima, Rio de Janeiro, Lisbon, Ankara, London, or Paris, the university library does not have to be very large. It can limit itself to the provision of books that the students are required to read in courses. In the United States, many of the largest and best-known universities, however, are in small cities, cities that do not have public libraries adequate for advanced study and research. In this case the university is obliged to have its own library or libraries.

An extensive university library system represents an enormous investment in time, money, and good will. It must support the research of the faculty and advanced students and the instruction of all the students, and it must also facilitate the specialized researcher's excursions into fields of knowledge adjacent to his own. On the research level it must support studies of the past — so-called retrospective research — and constantly fill in gaps in its collections. Next, it must support research that investigates present-day phenomena, natural and social, and keep as abreast as possible of an overwhelming production of books, pamphlets, documents, and learned reviews. Lastly, it must collect for the scholars of the future. Aware that no one library can do everything in even a single field, even for its own immediate clientele, a library system must constantly exercise sound judgments in its policies. It must always seek balance.

Operating a modern research library poses a series of problems. Two of great interest are the problems of cost and of space.

Book production in many countries is on a very large scale. With the expansion of universities and research institutes, learned reviews and books written by researchers have become more and more numerous. One explanation is the great competition that exists in the academic profession, with the result that scholars at times publish articles and books that are premature and even unnecessary in order to call attention to themselves and receive an invitation to a better institution. A university library should buy these journals and books; if it does so, it must catalogue them and store them. The cost of purchasing, cataloguing, and storing is high. What can be done about it?

Formerly it was thought that a university research library had to buy all the scholarly books published in the world. Today librarians realize that it is impossible to buy them all; they must be selective. Yet a librarian cannot selectively purchase books for all academic subjects; he needs faculty assistance. Unfortunately, each specialist on the faculty is inclined to recommend the purchase of all the books in his specialty. Such assistance is not very helpful. Consequently, the faculty should have a direct and immediate financial responsibility in the administration of the university library. In this way, the members of the faculty would know the facts concerning the administration of the library, especially the financial facts, and would hesitate to recommend the purchase of books which were not absolutely necessary.

In times past, all the great research libraries in the United States tried to buy as many books as possible. There was considerable unnecessary duplication. Now they all face the same financial difficulties and are entering into more interlibrary agreements. Thus they have actively entered into the so-called "Farmington plan," whereby the books published in various foreign countries are divided according to subject. One library agrees to buy *all* the books published by Farmington-plan countries in one subject, another library agrees to buy *all* the books published by these same countries in a second subject, and so' on. Researchers will consequently have within the United States at least one copy of each book of research value published since the respective country was included in the plan. There already exists a vast system of interlibrary loan and photographic reproduction. If, for example, the University of Minnesota Library has the reponsibility of buying all books on Scandinavian history, I can recommend to my library the purchase of a selected number, knowing full well that if I make a mistake or am not acquainted with a certain book, the Minneapolis library has all of them. If my university does not buy a book with whose title I am familiar and five years after its publication I need the book and cannot buy it because it is out of print, my university library borrows it from Minnesota for me.

Another type of interlibrary cooperation is represented by the regional library. So far, two patterns have emerged in the United States. On the one hand a "deposit library" occupies a relatively inexpensive building erected by a group of regularly established libraries in order to provide space for the storage of books that they are unable to store in their respective buildings. Space is rented out to the users, who retain title to their materials.

On the other hand, an "interlibrary center" is established to which the cooperating libraries send their lesser used materials. The center acquires title to these materials. In addition, it may have an acquisition program of its own.

Another important library problem is cataloguing, which is expensive and, perhaps of greater importance to the up-to-the-minute researcher, takes time. There are diverse opinions concerning cataloguing in a research library. One group believes there should be author, title, and subject cards. Another believes that only author cards are needed, since the specialist is already acquainted with the men working in his field and needs no other type of catalogue entry.

The complete and accurate description of a book in a library catalogue is difficult, requiring a trained cataloguer. Is such a complete description necessary? Opinions vary. Most scholars never trust a catalogue for a reference that they intend to cite in a publication and always quote from the book itself.

The Library of Congress in Washington is very helpful in the matter of cataloguing. It issues printed catalogue cards of books as they appear and other libraries may subscribe to the service, thus avoiding the trouble of making their own cards. Moreover, a library may acquire all the Library of Congress cards in order to have a catalogue of the books in and catalogued by the Library of Congress. A catalogue that includes cards on publications in the possession of other libraries is called a union catalogue.

Interlibrary cooperation in cataloguing is one of many examples of such cooperation. Other examples are furnished by such service as the production of specialized bibliographies.

Another problem, and a costly one for a research library, is the care of rare books and manuscripts, including their protection from bookworms, dust, humidity, fire, and heat, Not only are the acquisition and care of rare books costly but the continuing purchase of supporting modern studies of the individual rarities is a prime necessity for scholars. A collection of rare books cannot often be used in isolation.

As may be deduced from the foregoing, the administration of a large university library is complex. The personnel must be numerous and well trained. A university library could easily have over 200 employees. Many of its staff members of professional standing hold degrees from library schools in the United States. These schools are usually at the graduate level and have programs leading to both the master's and the doctor's degrees.

An American university is not exclusively a research center. It is also a teaching center. It has students. American students do not want to have the instruction that is imparted to them subordinated to the research of the teaching staff. They believe they have some claims on the university library. Therefore, a few words on the library from the point of view of the student, especially the undergraduate, are in order. As a generalization it is safe to say that American libraries are designed to be used, and are not archives or museums.

American undegraduates, with the possible exception of seniors, are often denied certain privileges in their university libraries that are enjoyed by graduate students. Thus the latter have the right to enter the stacks and get the books they wish. They can work at desks within the stacks. They may be assigned to such a desk for a year or more and keep the books they need right at the desk. The undergraduates in the same university cannot enter the stacks and browse among the books, selecting those that appeal to them and thus becoming familiar with many titles. They have to employ the catalogue, send for the book, and then wait, often for several minutes. They have to study in large and noisy reading rooms. One service is provided the undergraduates, on the other hand. Books that the professor requires the students of his course to consult may, if the course is large enough to warrant it, be gathered together by the library staff and "put on reserve" in one place.

Recognizing that one of the desired results of a college education is the pleasure derived from contact with books, American educators very much regret that the students in the university colleges do not have access to the stacks. Some universities have solved this problem by establishing libraries especially designed for the use of undergraduates. These libraries permit direct access to the stacks, for example, by requiring the students to pass through the stacks in order to reach the reading rooms. The reserved books are not grouped according to a theoretical and professional system of classification but according to the subjects studied by the students. The faculty of the university designates the books they wish to be included in the undergraduate library. It is thus completely functional. Moreover, the building may have air-conditioning, smoking rooms, typewriter booths, a phonograph-record or tape library, and many other features.

In addition to a central library, an American college or university may also maintain libraries in other buildings used by the students in an endeavor to make books a part of the very lives of the latter. And a faculty of course hopes that book ownership is widespread among its students.

It may not be inappropriate to add a few words concerning a serious problem intimately related to libraries. It is the problem of the publication of scholarly research and the role of uni-

versity presses. The cost of composition or type-setting is very high in the United States. Paper is expensive. Specialized books, however necessary for the progress of society, do not earn much money for commercial publishers. The large foundations hesitate to give money for publication. Consequently, researchers who devote months and years to a problem and the formulation of the results obtained often find publication well-nigh impossible. Here is where the university presses intervene and render assistance. These presses do not seek to make a profit; they are often subsidized by their respective universities, and are interested in scholarly publication. There are a large number of such presses, some of them quite old.

Even the university presses have financial difficulties, particularly those not subsidized by their parent institutions, and also the learned reviews, which are often published and financed by learned or professional societies. It is becoming increasingly necessary to familiarize researchers with new methods of reproduction, such as photo-offset and the micro-reproduction techniques that are less costly than normal printing, and advise them to be extremely careful in the preparation of their manuscripts, in the matters of quotations and footnotes, for example, so that the ultimate publication costs may be kept down. Indeed, in the courses taken by graduate students training is included in the preparation of manuscripts in accordance with the demands of modern times.

IX

Interuniversity Organization in the United States

IN THE United States there is no national or federal system of education, and consequently nothing corresponding to a Ministry of National Education. Education is the responsibility of the fifty states; within the states it is a responsibility of the cities and towns. Thus the public colleges and universities are state or municipal. There is no federal university as such, although such an institution has been proposed. Howard University, in the District of Columbia, however, has been federally aided since 1879. Established in 1867, it has devoted its attention primarily to the education of Negroes. It receives federal appropriations for maintenance and operation, with additional appropriations for buildings. Thus, by far the largest part of its budget is now from the federal government.

The latter government has, since the founding of the Republic, played an important role in stimulating the development of education. Perhaps the best-known example of federal legislation in support of education is the Morrill Act of 1862, which led to the establishment of the so-called "land-grant" colleges and universities. Grants of land were made to states provided emphasis would be placed on those branches of learning related to agriculture and the mechanic arts. Some of the land-grant institutions are state universities; others are separate state colleges of agriculture and mechanic arts.

Not only is there no official federal system of education, but there is no official interinstitutional organization. Within the executive branch of the federal government, however, there is the United States Office of Education, which is now part of the recently created Department of Health, Education, and Welfare, but it has little authority in educational matters; its function is limited to valuable statistical, informational, and advisory services, and to the implementation of federal legislation concerning education.

Some of the states, on the other hand, have an official interuniversity organization of the public or state universities. Indeed, in some states the public university system is a whole, well-organized entity. Thus, the state of Ohio has a state university in each corner of the state and one — the Ohio State University — in the center. The citizens of Ohio are very proud of the fact that there is a state university within short driving time of every home in the state. The state of New York has regrouped all of its public colleges and universities into a statewide system called the University of the State of New York. Such state interuniversity organizations are the only official organizations, and they include only the public institutions. They do not include private institutions, which are, however, chartered and, in a broad way, regulated by the state governments.

The reader might conclude that the lack of federal jurisdiction in education has been unduly emphasized. This emphasis has been made for two reasons.

The Constitution of the United States declares specifically that "the powers not delegated to the United States by the Constitution, nor prohibited by it to the States, are reserved to the States respectively, or to the people." In the United States the majority of the people wish, and always have wished, to maintain the autonomy of the states in matters of education. They do not want a federal system of education.

The second reason has already been developed in Chapter VI. Private institutions want to maintain their independence and want no government control, federal, state, or municipal. Moreover, private and public institutions are alike in wanting no federal control.

If there is in the United States no extensive official interuniversity organization, there is a voluntary system that is vast and complicated. There are free associations of institutions of higher education of many different types. Thus there is a series of regional educational associations of colleges and secondary schools — the Middle States Association, which includes the District of Columbia and Puerto Rico; the New England Association; the North Central Association; the Northwest Association, which includes Alaska; and the Southern Association. There is also a Western College Association. These associations determine their own conditions of membership. If a new college is established, one of the first things it does is seek membership in the appropriate regional association. The association admits it only after being assured that the new college satisfies all of the established requirements. If a college does not belong to its regional association, it has difficulty in attracting good students and, what is worse, its graduates often have great difficulty in gaining admission to graduate schools, which at times do not recognize the degrees awarded by such colleges. In other words, the association, by admitting a member, "accredits" that mem-

ber, to use the American terminology. Of interest in connection with the color problem in the South, to which reference was made in the first chapter, is the action taken in 1957 by the Southern Association of Colleges and Secondary Schools to abolish distinctions in membership between Negro and white colleges by 1961.

This accreditation service has in the past been most useful in maintaining a certain uniformity and high standards in the instruction offered by American colleges. In general, however, the concept of accreditation has one great defect. In a country like the United States, with the widespread diversity among its institutions of higher education, accreditation can actually impede progress in education by being too conservative. Consequently, accreditation seems to be less favorably regarded now than formerly.

In a certain sense, accreditation is a contradiction in the American system. Higher education in the United States is free of national, governmental control. Different types of institutions are legally free to develop as they deem appropriate, each type serving a special need. Ironically, however, the very educators who enjoy this freedom and are proud of it enter voluntarily into restrictive arrangements, always in the name of high standards, to be sure. The result is that, in the United States, as was pointed out at the beginning of Chapter IV, there is a surprising degree of non-compulsory uniformity in higher education.

Of the many four-year institutions at the level of higher education, less than a thousand are accredited. Those that are not accredited, and it is estimated that they may number 500, feel that, with the proper assistance, especially financial aid, they can improve themselves and play an important role in meeting the anticipated swollen enrollment of the next few years. In 1956 some of them joined together and formed a Council for the Advancement of Small Colleges in order to make their plight and their potentialities better known.

In addition to the regional educational associations there is a national association of universities, national but voluntary, of few members and of considerable prestige. It is the Association of American Universities (A.A.U.), composed of forty-one universities of the United States and Canada (but not of Mexico), including the Massachusetts Institute of Technology and the California Institute of Technology. A new member can be admitted only with the approval of three-quarters of the membership. Membership requirements are high, the quality of the graduate schools being the principal criterion. It should be added that the Association of American Universities has no authority over any of its members, although agreements reached at annual meetings are felt to be morally binding.

The Association of American Universities formerly maintained an accrediting service. It kept a list of approved colleges, universities, and technological institutions whose qualified graduates were admitted to graduate schools of the association. It abandoned the service in 1948.

In the United States, in addition to the Association of American Universities, there are many voluntary national associations of specific types of institutions, as, for example, the Association of American Colleges, American Association of Colleges for Teacher Education, American Association of Land-Grant Colleges and State Universities, Association of Urban Universities, National Association of State Universities, Association of American Law Schools, and Association of American Medical Colleges. In addition, there are regional functional associations, like the New England Conference on Graduate Education.

So far only associations of institutions have been mentioned. There are also, in the United States, a large number of educational associations composed of individuals, for instance, the American Association of Collegiate Registrars and Admissions Officers and the National Association of Student Personnel Administrators and the American Association of University Women (A.A.U.W.). These associations have regular meetings, often an annual meeting; the individuals who attend discuss their problems and thus contribute to the improvement of the educational system, freely, without government intervention.

For relations with the federal government, as well as for many other reasons, the various educational institutions and associations maintain in the city of Washington the American Council on Education (A.C.E.), whose permanent secretariat, among other duties, studies legislation concerning or affecting educational matters under consideration by the Congress and expresses the opinions of the members of the Council to the members of Congress, a democratic and effective procedure.

Another national organization of considerable importance in the influencing of public opinion is the National Education Association, whose membership is individual. Its Association for Higher Education is very active.

There are two national American organizations that are of great interest to the foreign reader who might wish to study in the United States. The first is the U.S. Office of Education, already mentioned at the beginning of this chapter. The second is the Institute of International Education (I.I.E.), whose headquarters is in New York City. Founded in 1919, the I.I.E. is most important for foreign students. It is an independent private institute financed by contributions from many sources, including contributions from foundations and from individual educational institutions. Its personnel are both able and willing and perform a truly extraordinary service for foreign students in the United States and for American students abroad. The Institute has the support and confidence of American colleges and universities, of the United States government, and of foreign governments. Its role in international student exchange is discussed in the following chapter.

Another group of associations of great importance for American education are the learned societies, which are free and voluntary national associations of individuals concerned with a specific academic discipline and may or may not be selective in their membership. Examples are the American Psychological Association, the American Chemical Society, the Linguistic Society of America, and the Modern Language Association of America. As a general rule, each learned society has an annual meeting and publishes a review or journal which contains articles, book reviews, lists of books received, personalia, and the like. The learned societies are in touch with similar societies in other countries and are most important for the development of the respective specialties. In addition to their purely scientific role, the societies and their journals have a practical one, the placement of personnel, as mentioned in Chapter V.

Americans seem to have a genius for organization. Not content with all of the preceding, including an enormous number of learned societies, they organize what are in effect associations of learned societies, the American Council of Learned Societies for the humanities (and also history and certain other fields), and the Social Research Council for the social sciences; for the natural sciences the National Research Council, although not an association of learned societies, has representation from them. American organizational genius is not yet exhausted. There is also a Conference Board of Associated Research Councils which also includes the American Council on Education.

Two more associations should be mentioned in any list of interuniversity organizations in the United States. One is the American Association of University Professors, whose role in American education is discussed in Chapter V. If professors can organize, so can the students. Therefore there is, for example, the National Student Association, which, like the A.A.U.P., has chapters in many universities.

A movement among universities which began in the southern part of the United States is of great interest and significance for the future, for it suggests a solution to many financial problems. In the United States there are so many universities that it is impossible for each one to be outstanding in every field. Indeed, a university must be selective in the fields that it supports and must try to do well what it undertakes to do, but it must not attempt to do too much. If one university does not have courses in a given subject that are desired or needed by a student, the university should, and in fact often does, send him to another institution for a short time to get these courses. This type of cooperation is now quite extensive in the South, where the governments of thirteen states agreed in 1949 to evolve a cooperative system of education and so established the Southern Regional Education Board. In July 1950 a meeting of the representatives of the universities of these states was held in Florida to decide which specialties each university should develop. The Board, which now represents fourteen states ranging from Maryland to Texas, has been very active.

This regional movement in the South is especially important for medical education. It is impossible for each southern state to have good medical schools. If some states take care of the training of physicians, others can do other things, and costs will thus be distributed. This is a perfect example of interuniversity organization that is interstate but not federal. It has borne fruit in both the western and northeastern parts of the United States, and thirty-five states now belong to regional groupings. The New England Board of Higher Education was organized in 1955. By 1957 all six New England states had joined. They meet the administrative costs in proportion to their population. The purpose of the Board is to increase opportunities in higher education for New England residents through regional cooperation. It is particularly interested in the preparation of college teachers.

Although regional cooperation is relatively new, local cooperation is old. For many years graduate students at Harvard and the Massachusetts Institute of Technology have been permitted to take up to half their courses in the other institution. There has been a similar "cross-registration" agreement among the Harvard Divinity School, Boston University School of Theology, Andover Newton Theological School, and Tufts University Theological School.

The pattern of local cooperation is inevitably spreading. In the Connecticut River Valley of Massachusetts the University of Massachusetts (public) and Amherst College, Mount Holyoke College, and Smith College (all private) have banded together to solve many mutual problems, especially the elimination of duplication.

A most imaginative plan, deserving of the highest praise, was very recently announced by Syracuse University. Eight major universities (Syracuse, Chicago, Cornell, Indiana, Michigan, Northwestern, Pennsylvania, and Tulane) are collaborating in a "wandering scholar" program covering three years of study of Italian language and literature and leading to the Ph.D., the degree to be granted by the university under whose guidance the graduate student writes his thesis.

X

American Colleges and Universities
and International Student Exchange

KNOWLEDGE, science, research, and truth are international. A university is therefore necessarily international. In the United States the great universities have been international in their outlook from the time they were founded. Since

World War II in particular, the smaller universities and the independent colleges, fully conscious of their responsibilities in a world but recently torn by strife of gigantic proportions, have made an enormous effort to attract and to take care of foreign students. Indeed, they may perhaps be criticized for being too kind to foreign students. When these students arrive, the officers and students of these institutions often do too much in their desire to be hospitable. They tend to place the foreign students in a special category instead of letting them study and live freely like the American students. This is a defect that American educators have recognized and are remedying.

During the academic year 1958–1959 there were 47,245 foreign students in the United States from 131 different countries. The distribution of their interests is significant. The most popular subject was engineering, with 10,682 students. Next came the humanities (9,472), within which theology is included (2,342). The natural and physical sciences followed (6,737), then the social sciences (6,432), business administration (3,952), the medical sciences (3,765), education (2,340), and agriculture (1,632). Apparently more students come to the United States to study theology than agriculture or education!

Of the 47,245 foreign students, 24,349 were in undergraduate colleges.

Of the 47,245 students, about 27,668 or 58.3 per cent, received financial aid from an American institution, from the United States Government, from the student's government, or from an institution in the student's country.

The University of California had the largest number of foreign students of all American institutions, with a total of 1,693. The Massachusetts Institute of Technology traditionally has the highest percentage of foreign students 12.4 per cent in 1958–1959).

The above statistics, which give an idea of the magnitude of American participation in international student exchange, were furnished by the Institute of International Education, whose excellent work has already been mentioned in Chapter IX. The Institute administers a large number of scholarships and coordinates the award of several small scholarships to one individual. It has little money of its own to award, but it does the administrative work for other institutions and organizations. In addition to handling scholarships, it helps the foreign student to gain admission by forwarding his papers to an appropriate American institution.

The great universities of the world want the movement of intellectuals to be free; they want that often-forgotten freedom which was once possessed by the world, freedom of movement. The obstacles in the way are not caused by universities. They are caused by extra-educational forces, such as language and financial difficulties.

An American always has a certain hesitation in calling the attention of foreign students to the necessity of their learning English in order to study in the United States, for he realizes full well that the knowledge of foreign languages on the part of American students abroad often leaves much to be desired. Unfortunately, however, American colleges and universities as a general rule cannot accept foreign students who do not know English for normal programs during the academic year. They do not ordinarily have special programs for such students, as does, for example, the University of Paris. As was mentioned in Chapter II, they do have a series of summer schools that offer special English courses for foreigners. The foreign student who wants to follow a regular program during the normal academic year (September to June) may come to the United States at the beginning of the July preceding that academic year in order to devote two months of summer-school work to the English language. Unfortunately, attendance at such a summer school would increase the period of residence in the United States by about three months. If the student does not have sufficient funds for a full twelve months, he is perhaps better advised to perfect his English in advance in his own country.

If the male student is accompanied by his wife, she should also learn English. If not, the two will speak their native language at home and he will not make rapid progress in English. Moreover, the wife will need English for her housekeeping duties.

The possibility of the foreign student's earning money during the period of his study in the United States depends on the nature of the visa that he has. In general, students have, logically enough, a "student," or F visa. Students possessing this visa may, under present government regulations, work on a part-time basis with the permission of the immigration authorities, but normally not during their first year of study. They may work full-time during the summer vacation provided they continue their studies the following term. On receipt of a degree and on the recommendation of their American institution, they may receive practical training and experience in their field of study for a period of six months for each academic year of study spent in the United States, up to a maximum of eighteen months. During the academic year all foreign students with an F visa must pursue studies at the full-time rate. In other words, if they have to work, this employment cannot interfere with their normal progress within the program in which they are registered.

Wives accompanying husbands usually travel under a "tourist," or B-2 visa, which permits no paid employment whatsoever.

If a student enters the United States with a permanent residence visa, he will encounter no governmental restrictions as far as work is concerned. From the point of view of his studies, however, this visa has one great defect: its possessor is subject to possible military service in the armed forces of the United States.

Some governments feel obliged to restrict the amount of currency that their nationals may take abroad. As far as American colleges and universities are concerned, it is far more satisfactory to make a detailed certification to the foreign government of what the necessary expenses in the United States will be than to have that government set an arbitrary limit which bears little relation to student expenses in the United States. American institutions are very conscientious in making such certification and do not include the price of luxury items as a necessary expense.

The foreign student's life in an American institution of higher education depends on his own efforts, although, as has been noted, American colleges and universities aid him to a considerable degree. Some institutions have active clubs and even "international houses" for foreign students. Other institutions prefer to treat foreign students as Americans.

The majority of the larger American universities have a foreign-student adviser, who plays an important role in helping the student with financial problems, room, board, visas, and general government regulations. The importance of these advisers is such that they have a National Association of Foreign Student Advisers whose annual meeting attracts considerable attention.

Foreign students often worry, perhaps unnecessarily, about the vexing problems of "credits" and the equivalence of degrees. In accordance with the general American educational philosophy, foreign students are often studied individually and are placed in appropriate courses with little reference to the credits or diplomas previously acquired by them. This course placement carried out by American institutions is based on their rather extensive experience in the past and, in general, can be relied on as very fair. The whole matter of the equivalence of degrees is one to which the International Association of Universities, with headquarters in Paris, has addressed itself.

So far in this chapter only foreign students in the United States have been discussed. As for American students abroad, the tradition of study in foreign countries, especially in European countries, is very strong in the United States. Formerly, the wealthy student completed his studies by devoting a year or more to the grand tour, France, Switzerland, Italy, Germany, England, possibly the Iberian peninsula. The Mecca, of course, was Paris. Today American students generally go abroad with much more specific purposes; their studies abroad are usually carefully integrated with those completed in the United States.

The majority of American students who attend foreign universities are graduate students, usually of the arts and sciences. They go abroad to do research. They study manuscripts, other documents, works of art, and so forth. They seek to acquire fluency in languages. Very often the work that they do is the core of the Ph.D. thesis.

Since 1923 a most significant experiment in foreign study has been conducted on a limited basis, the study abroad of American college juniors. Normally the American undergraduate cannot attend a foreign university during regular sessions for two reasons. First, foreign universities would not admit him because they deem him too young. Inasmuch as he is nineteen, twenty, or twenty-one years of age, the real reason is probably that they consider him too immature. Second, if the American undergraduate went abroad to study, his home college would not count the year among the four required for the bachelor's degree. His college takes this attitude for a variety of reasons, probably an important one being that it fears he will only frequent cafés and the Folies Bergères and do little studying.

Yet the idea of an American undergraduate's studying abroad, knowing different countries and different ways of thinking, acquiring an excellent working knowledge of a second language, as an integral part of the bachelor's program, without the loss of a year, is an excellent one. Therefore, almost forty years ago arrangements were made with the University of Paris whereby a small group of highly qualified American juniors could study in France. The success of this first group, which was originally organized by the University of Delaware and is still operating, under the auspices of Sweet Briar College in Virginia, was enormous. Now there are several such groups, not only in France, but also in Brazil, Germany, Italy, Mexico,

Spain, and Switzerland. Each group has from ten or fifteen to eighty or ninety students.

The model of the junior-year groups, which are small, homogeneous, and well organized, has penetrated graduate study abroad. Middlebury College, long famed for its foreign-language summer schools in the state of Vermont, has graduate groups in France, Germany, and Spain and awards a master's degree for the year of foreign study.

In my opinion, if we are to have one world living in peace with itself, more young students must live abroad. Young students willingly tolerate the changes in habit and the inconveniences that travel inevitably entails. They learn languages rapidly. They are not preoccupied with specialization; they stay out of libraries and archives and see all sides of life in the foreign country. They do not have any great dignity or prestige to maintain and can burrow into all corners of the foreign country; when they return home, they are much less apt to use the clichés and generalizations that older students and other intellectuals often come to use after travel abroad later in life. For these reasons I strongly favor the junior-year-abroad programs.

The international exchange not only of students but also of teachers, educational administrators, and professional persons of all sorts has increased significantly since the end of World War II. American colleges and universities participate actively in the exchange because they recognize the benefits not only to international understanding but also to the improvement of educational systems. They are particularly desirous of exchanging information so that higher education in the United States may be known abroad and may be constantly modified in accordance with experience gained abroad.

Index

A. A. U. *See* Association of American Universities

A. A. U. P. *See* American Association of University Professors

Acceleration, 14, 29

Accreditation, 55, 61, 62

A. C. E. *See* American Council on Education

Achievement tests, 14

Adjunct in Arts, degree of, 14

Admission, 1, 2, 5, 7, 9, 12, 16, 22, 25, 26, 31, 43, 50, 52, 53, 54, 56, 61, 65, 67

Admission without Diploma, 30

Adult education, 14

Advanced Placement, 30

Advancement. *See* Promotion

Advanced Standing, 17, 30, 52

Adviser, foreign student, 67

Advising, 10, 26

Agriculture, 7, 50, 60, 65

Alma mater, 20

Alumni (*or* alumnae), 12, 13, 20, 47

American Association of University Professors, 44, 63

American College Fund, 48

American Council of Learned Societies, 63

American Council on Education, 62, 63

Appointment office. *See* Placement of students in positions

Apprentice teaching. *See* Practice teaching

Aptitude, 25

Aptitude tests, 14, 26

Architecture, 7, 53

Assistant, 47

Assistant professor, 32, 41, 42, 43

Associate in Arts, degree of, 21

Associate professor, 32, 41

Association of American Universities, 62

Athletics, 14, 15, 20, 21

Attendance, compulsory, 2

Audio-visual aids, 18, 28

Aural-oral, 18, 26

Baccalaureate. *See* Bachelor's degree

Bachelor of Architecture, degree of, 54

Bachelor of Arts, degree of, 5, 15, 22, 51

Bachelor of Laws, degree of, 53

Bachelor of Science, degree of, 5, 15, 22, 51

Bachelor's degree, 7, 8, 17, 19, 23, 26, 27, 28, 31, 50, 51, 52, 53, 54, 55, 67

Bar examination, 53

Beneficiary aid funds, 49

Big sister (i. e., student adviser), 10

Blue-book (i. e., examination book), 19

Board. *See* Dining hall

Board of trustees, 11, 12, 48

Budget, 10, 46, 48, 49

Buildings and grounds, 13

Business Administration, 7, 8, 54, 65

Cap and gown, 20

Case method, 18, 54

Cataloguing, library, 57

Chair (i. e., professorship), 41, 47

Chairman, Department, 10, 13, 43, 49; *see also* Head, Department

Chancellor, 11

Chapel, 29, 49

Chaplain, 28

Charter, State, 12, 45, 60

Cheating, 19

Choice of courses, Freedom of, 13, 17, 23

Church institutions, 2, 7, 18, 19, 23, 44

Civil rights, 55

Class standing, 19

Closed-circuit television, 28

Clubs, 15, 16, 20

   for foreign students, 66

Coed, 17

Coeducation, 17, 26, 56

College, English, 1, 16

Collège, French, 8

College of arts and sciences. *See* College of liberal arts

College of liberal arts, 7 and *passim*

College program, 7

Commencement (i. e., end of studies), 20, 49, 54

Commerce. *See* Business administration

Commission, Reserve officer's, 55

Committee, 10, 11, 26

Community college, 2, 21, 22

Commuters, 16

Concentration, 23, 25

Conference Board of Associated Research Councils, 63

Consultant, 11, 42

Contractual research, 48

Control, government, 19, 22, 46, 48, 61

Corporate giving, 48

Council for the Advancement of Small Colleges, 62

Council, student, 13

Counsel, study, 14
Counselor, 10
Course, 6, 13, 17, 18, 19, 23, 26, 32, 51, 56, 63, 67
Creative arts, 26
Credit hour, 17
Credits, 17, 67
Cross-registration, 64
Curriculum, 4, 13, 16, 22ff., 52

Dean, 8, 9, 10, 13, 21, 43, 48
Debating, 15
Defense of thesis, 32
Degree, academic, 10, 13, 14, 15, 20, 61
Dental medicine, 8, 55
Department (of a faculty), 10, 11, 42, 43, 48, 49
Department of Health, Education, and Welfare, 60
Deposit library, 57
Design. *See* Architecture
Dining hall, 2, 15, 16, 21, 22
Diploma, 50, 55, 67
Discrimination, 1, 61
Dissertation. *See* Thesis
Distribution, 23
Divinity school. *See* Ministry
Division (of a faculty), 10
Doctorate, 7, 8, 32, 52, 58
Doctor of Medicine, degree of, 52
Doctor of Philosophy, degree of, 31, 32, 43, 64, 67
Dormitory, 2, 15, 16, 20, 49
Dramatics, 15, 20, 26

Education (i. e., pedagogy), 8, 11, 14, 31, 51, 65
Electives, free, 17, 23
Elementary school, 2, 4, 7, 21, 22, 25, 26, 27, 30, 41, 50, 51
Emeritus professor, 44
Employment, student, 21, 29, 66
Endowment, 45, 46, 49
Engineering, 7, 19, 30, 42, 50, 52, 54, 55, 65
English for foreigners, 14, 65
Equality of opportunity, 1, 5, 6, 25
Equivalence of degrees, 67
Examination, 10, 11, 18, 19, 53, 55
Executive officer, 10; *see also* Chairman, Department
Expenses, student, 20, 66
Extension, university, 14, 42
Extracurricular activities, 15, 20

Faculty, 8 and *passim*
of arts and sciences, 9, 11, 31
Farmington plan, 57
Federal government, 2, 12, 17, 19, 22, 44, 45, 46, 48, 60, 61, 63, 65

Fees, student, 20, 45; *see also* Tuition
Fellowships (often larger in amount than scholarships, i. e., covering more than tuition), 2, 11, 20, 21, 32, 42, 46, 49
Field of concentration, 19, 23, 51
Field trip, 18
Football, 14
Foreign languages, 4, 5, 24, 25, 26, 27, 65, 68
Foundations, philanthropic, 12, 32, 42, 47, 59, 63
Fraternity, 16
Free-elective system, 23
Freedom, academic, 12, 44, 46
Freshman (i. e., first-year college student), 10, 20, 30
Fringe benefits, 41
Full professor, 32, 41
Full-time, 32, 42, 66

General education, 5, 9, 23, 24, 28, 31, 50, 52
General examination, 19, 32
G. I. Bill, 2
Gifts for immediate use, 45, 46
Governing board (e. g., board of trustees), 12
Government, 11, 12, 22, 31, 42, 44, 45, 46, 48, 62; *see also* Federal Government
Grades (i. e., marks), 19, 26
Grades in elementary school, 51
Graduate program, 7, 30, 31, 32
Graduate school, 5, 7, and *passim*
of arts and sciences, *passim*
of education, 3, 51
Graduate student, 9, 15, 22, 31
Graduates (i. e., alumni), 13, 62
Grammar school, 22
Grandmother (i. e., student adviser), 10
Grants, 47
"Great books," 24
Greek-letter society. *See* Fraternity, Honor society, Sorority
Gymnasium, German, 8
Gymnasiums, 49

Head, Department, 10, 43; *see also* Chairman, Department
Health, 22, 29
High school, 5, 7, 22, 24, 25, 27, 29, 30, 50
Higher education assistance corporation, 21
Home economics, 7, 26
Honor society, 19
Honorary degrees, 49
Honors, degrees with, 19
House system, 16, 18
Houses, International, 66
Housing, faculty, 31, 41
Human relations, 26, 54

I. I. E. *See* Institute of International Education
Income, 45

Industry, 11, 12, 31, 42, 43, 46, 47, 48, 54
Institute of International Education, 63, 65
of technology, 7, 52, 62; *see also* Technological college
Instructor, 32, 41, 42
Instructional laboratory, 18
Insurance, life, 41
Integration, 25, 67
Interdisciplinary programs, 11, 32
Interlibrary center, 57
International Association of Universities, 67
International Legal Studies, 53
Interneship, 52
Intramural sports, 20

Journal, learned, *See* Learned review
Journalism, 55
Junior (i. e., third-year college student), 10, 20, 23, 67
Junior college, 2, 8, 22
Junior high school, 3, 7, 22
Junior year abroad, 67, 68

Kindergarten, 2

Laboratory, 2, 13, 17, 18, 45, 49
Land-grant institutions, 60, 62
Language laboratory, 18
Language requirement, 27
Law, 7, 8, 18, 22, 30, 41, 53, 54, 55, 62
Learned review, 56, 59, 63
Lecture, noncourse, 20 42
Lecture system, 9, 17, 18
Letter of recommendation, 11
Liberal-arts college. *See* College of liberal arts
Library, 2, 13, 16, 21, 45, 47, 49, 56ff., 68
Library school, 58
Licensing, professional, 19, 55
LL. B. *See* Bachelor of Laws
Loan, interlibrary, 57
Loan funds, 21, 45, 49
Lodgings. *See* Dormitory
Lower division, 8
Lycée, 8

Major. *See* Field of concentration
Marking, 19
Master, house, 16
Master in Architecture, degree of, 54
Master in Business Administration, degree of, 54
Master's degree, 7, 8, 51, 52, 58, 68
M. B. A. *See* Master in Business Administration
M. D. *See* Doctor of Medicine
Mechanic arts, 60
Medical plan (for faculty), 41
Medical service (for students), 2, 13, 45

Medicine, 5, 7, 8, 11, 22, 30, 41, 52, 53, 54, 55, 56, 62, 64, 65
Micro-reproduction, 59
Military profession, 54
Military service, 29, 66
Ministry (i. e., clergy), 7, 11, 51, 54
Ministry of National Education, 19, 60
Mission of a university, 11
Money raising, 13, 46
Morrill Act of 1862, 60
Museums, 49
Music, 7, 15, 26

National Defense Education Act of 1958, 25
National Education Association, 62
National Research Council, 63
National Science Foundation, 46
National Student Association, 63
New England Board of Higher Education, 64
New England Colleges Fund, 48
Normal school, 50
Nursery school, 1, 22
Nursing, 7

Office of Education, U. S., 2, 50, 63
Oral examinations, 19, 32
Overseers, 12

Pedagogy. *See* Education
Pension, 41, 44
Permanent residence visa, 66
Ph. D. *See* Doctor of Philosophy
Philanthropy, 6, 12, 46, 49
Physical education, 7
Physical exercise, 14, 15
Placement of students in courses, 14, 26, 67
of students in positions, 10, 13, 41, 43, 63
Placement tests, 14, 26
Points. *See* Credits
Polls, opinion, 13, 43
Popularization, 9, 42
Postdoctoral research, 32
Practice teaching, 9, 15, 18, 32, 51
Preceptor, 20
Premedical program, 52
Preparatory school, 3, 25, 51
Preprofessional preparation, 23, 50
Prerequisites, 25
President (of a college or university), 11, 12, 48
Press, university, 59
Primary school, 22
Professional training, 4, 7, 8, 42, 47, 65ff.
Professor, 8, 32, and *passim*
Promotion (of faculty members), 10, 41, 43
Public health, 8
Publication, 31, 43, 56, 59

Quarter (of a year), 14

Rank (i. e., class standing), 19
Ranks, academic, 32
Rector, 11
Recruitment, 42
Regents, 12
Regional library, 57
Registrar, 12, 62
Religion, 11, 15, 28, 29, 49
Research, 4, 9, 11, 18, 19, 30, 31, 32, 42, 47, 48, 52, 56, 58, 59, 64, 67
Research contracts, 48
Research institutes, 56
Reserve Officers Training Corps, 55
Reserved books, 59
Residence requirement, 32
Retirement, 44
Roommate, 16
R. O. T. C. See Reserve Officers Training Corps
Royalties, 42

Sabbatical leave, 41
Salaries, 13, 15, 28, 31, 32, 41, 42, 43, 44, 45, 47, 48, 49, 50, 51
Scholarships (often smaller in amount than fellowships, i. e., covering tuition or less), 2, 11, 13, 20, 21, 41, 45, 46, 47, 49, 53, 65
Secondary school, 2, 4, 11, 21, 25, 26, 27, 30, 41, 50, 51, 52, 54
Secretarial college, 26
Segregation, 2
Semester, 17, 19
Semester hour, 17
Seminar, 18, 32
Seminary. See Ministry
Senior (i. e., fourth-year college student), 20, 23, 41, 58
Small colleges, 62
Social Science Research Council, 63
Social Security, 44
Social work, 7
Societies, learned, 59, 63
    professional, 55, 59
Sophomore (i. e., second-year college student), 20, 23, 30
Sophomore Standing, 30
Sorority, 16
Southern Regional Education Board, 64
Sports, 20; see also Athletics
Stacks, library, 58, 59
Standards, 4, 5, 61
States rights, 45, 60
Student visa, 66
Subject matter, 4, 9, 14, 26
Summer school, 14, 29, 42, 51, 66
Syllabus, 18

Tape-recorders, 18, 26, 59
Tax, income, 45, 46
    inheritance, 45
    real estate, 46
Teachers college, 3, 50, 51
Teachers Insurance and Annuity Association, 44
Teaching Assistant, 32
Teaching Fellow, 32
Technological college, 7, 50; see also Institute of technology
Technical institute. See Institute of technology
Television, 14, 20, 26, 28
Tenure, life, 12, 41, 44
Term, 17
Terminal education, 5
Testing, 14
Textbooks, 9, 42
Theology, 28, 65; see also Ministry
Thesis, 19, 32, 64, 67
T. I. A. A. See Teachers Insurance and Annuity Association
Tourist visa, 66
Town and gown, 16
Transcript, 26
Transfer-student, 17
Traveling fellowship, 47
Treasurer, 48, 49
Trustees. See Board of trustees
Tuition, 6, 20, 21, 45, 46, 49, 53
Tuition Plan, 21
Tutor, 19, 20, 21
Tutorial schools, 14

Undergraduate college, 7, 22, 47, 50
Undergraduate student, 9, 18, 22, 31
Union (i. e., student center), 20
Union, teachers', 43
Union catalogue, 58
University, definition of, 7
University college, 5, 7, 18, 31
Upperclassmen, 20

Vacation, 17, 20, 66
Veterans, War, 2, 46
Vice-President (of a college or university), 48
Visa, 66, 67
Vocational college, 50
Vocational guidance, 13, 26, 41
Vocational school, 3

Wandering scholar program, 64
Women, 10, 15, 16, 17, 20, 26, 31, 55, 62
Woodrow Wilson Fellowships, 42

Year, academic, 15, 66